T0131535

GENIUS OF THE TRANSCENDENT

GENIUS OF THE TRANSCENDENT

Mystical Writings of
JAKOB BOEHME

Translated by
Michael L. Birkel and Jeff Bach

Shambhala
Boulder
2010

Shambhala Publications, Inc.
4720 Walnut Street
Boulder, Colorado 80301
www.shambhala.com

Printed in the United States of America

♾ This edition is printed on acid-free paper that meets the
American National Standards Institute z39.48 Standard.
♻ Shambhala Publications makes every effort to print on recycled paper.
For more information please visit www.shambhala.com.
Distributed in the United States by Penguin Random House LLC
and in Canada by Random House of Canada Ltd

Designed by James D. Skatges

Library of Congress Cataloging-in-Publication Data
Böhme, Jakob, 1575–1624.
[Selections. English. 2010]
Genius of the transcendent: mystical writings of Jakob Boehme /
translated by Michael L. Birkel and Jeff Bach.—1st ed.
p. cm.
Includes bibliographical references (p.   ).
ISBN 978-1-59030-709-0 (pbk.: alk. paper)
1. Mysticism. 2. Theology, Doctrinal. I. Birkel, Michael Lawrence.
II. Bach, Jeff, 1958– III. Title.
BV5095.B7A25 2010
248.2'2—dc22
2009034485

To our families

Contents

Acknowledgments

This book began through friendships, formed by our daughters in middle school and between us through professional contacts and through a reading group for biblical Hebrew during the time when both our families lived in Indiana. As we learned more about each other's research interests—Michael's in the Religious Society of Friends (or Quakers) and Jeff's in Radical Pietism and the Church of the Brethren—we discovered that both the Friends and the Brethren had early exposure to Jakob Boehme. This book grew out of a shared interest in finding out more about Boehme and our traditions, the Quakers and the Brethren. We thank our daughters, Anna Margaret Birkel and Rebecca Bach, for starting the connections. We are also grateful to our friends in the Hebrew reading group: Nancy Bowen, Gordon Thompson, and Robert Southard (ז״ל).

This project intends to present selections from Boehme's writings in a way that introduces readers to some of his world of symbol and spirituality. Discerning readers may at times identify two distinct voices in this book. As collaborators we thank one another for giving each other permission to interpret Boehme in his own theological idiom. The texts include some accessible selections and some that represent the wider range of Boehme's complexity. Ultimately we tried out this process in an academic course. To the students who joined us for this experiment in spring 2006 at Earlham College, Bethany Theological Seminary, and Earlham School of Religion, all in Richmond, Indiana, we extend our thanks.

We began our reading of Jakob Boehme with the copy of the 1730 edition of his complete works, which is housed in the Abraham Harley Cassel Collection of Bethany Theological Seminary in the archives of Lilly Library at Earlham College. We thank our colleagues there, especially Thomas Hamm and Michelle Riggs (since departed for Louisiana) and Christine Larson, formerly the theological librarian at Lilly Library. The interlibrary loan departments at both Elizabethtown College and Earlham College also receive our gratitude. For technical assistance in handling the text of this book in various stages, we thank Hillary Daecher, administrative assistant at the Young Center for Anabaptist and Pietist Studies at Elizabethtown College, and Deanna Airgood, administrative assistant for the religion and philosophy departments at Earlham College. Michael thanks Earlham College for the sabbatical leave that freed him to work on this project, and his son Jonathan for computer guidance.

Finally, we are thankful to our editors at Shambhala Publications: David O'Neal for his advocacy of this project and his supportive guidance, and Chloe Foster for her expert care. May all these people, and the readers of this book, experience the joy that Jakob Boehme wrote about.

GENIUS OF THE
TRANSCENDENT

INTRODUCTION

*If you can swing yourself up for a moment into that in which
no creature dwells, then you will you hear what God speaks.*

*If you keep silent from sensing and willing of your self, then the
eternal hearing, seeing, and speaking will be revealed within you.*

*If you would remain silent, then you are what God was before
nature and creatureliness.*

WITH THESE PROMISING WORDS and exacting challenges, we are invited into the rich and complex cosmos of
Jakob Boehme: the humble shoemaker of Görlitz, Bohemia; a mystic, prophet, and self-taught theosophist. Each generation since his
time has found its own way into his compelling vision of the inward
life, and this volume aspires to present some of his words afresh for
the present generation of spiritual seekers.

Boehme's Illumination

The person of Jakob Boehme is as compelling as his writings, even if any portrait of him is a mixture of facts and uncertainties, both of which were supplied by his disciple and biographer, Abraham von Franckenberg. We know that Boehme entered this world in 1575 in Alt-Seidenberg, a village near the city of Görlitz, the fourth of five children born to Jakob and Ursula Boehme, who were free peasants. They were prosperous enough to obtain some elementary schooling for their son and to apprentice him to a cobbler, a trade that the younger Jakob followed until his later years when he closed his shop and entered the linen trade. Less reliable, perhaps, are the stories about a visitation from a stranger who foretold greatness for Jakob when he was a young apprentice.

Both Boehme and his biographer wrote of a turning point in Boehme's life, an experience of spiritual illumination. Franckenberg's account tells of a vision, inspired by the brilliance of sunlight reflected from a pewter dish. This radiance opened to the young Boehme the inner secrets of the natural and divine worlds, and this feeling of illumination only intensified as he walked out into the countryside, where the natural world confirmed his experience. Boehme was twenty-five years old at the time of this experience, and he continued to ply his craft as a shoemaker without writing anything about his illumination. Twelve years later another inner experience convinced him that he must commit his insights to writing, though he later acknowledged that he did not expect his writing would be read by anyone other than himself.

Boehme's own description of this initial turning point is at once less and more dramatic than Franckenberg's account. It mentions neither the pewter vessel nor the radiant beam. Instead, as he wrote in a letter twelve years later:

> I saw and knew more in one quarter of an hour than if I had spent many years at a university. I saw and recognized the

Being of All Beings, the foundation and that which is beyond foundation and is fathomless. I saw the birth of the Holy Threeness of God, the origin and primordial condition of this world and all creatures through divine wisdom. I saw and knew the three worlds: the first being divine, angelic, and paradisiacal; the second being the dark-world, the primordial condition of the nature of fire; and the third being this outward, visible world, as a creation and offspring birthed and spoken forth from the first two inward and spiritual worlds.[1]

When Boehme broke his literary silence by writing his first book, he described this decisive experience in terms of the divine love that he encountered after a difficult struggle with melancholy:

> After a number of violent storms, my spirit broke through the gates of hell, into the innermost birth of the Godhead, where it was embraced with love, as a bridegroom embraces his beloved bride.[2]

As the gates of hell broke open, so did a veritable deluge of words, and Boehme dedicated the rest of his life to an attempt to give expression to his experiences. Not only was it striking that a humble cobbler should claim such extraordinary experiences, but it was equally astonishing that so many pages should pour forth from the hand of a son of peasants. To those who considered themselves his social superiors, Boehme was an uneducated provincial, and frankly unworthy of the profound insight that he alleged to have. *Aurora*, his first major work, brought him into conflict with church authorities, who ordered him to cease writing. Boehme states that he dutifully observed this silence as long as he could, and then a torrent of words poured forth in his final years. These later writings are the focus of this volume.

His Legacy

Boehme's works found an appreciative if limited circle of readers during his lifetime, and since then his writings have gone on to influence countless readers over the centuries. Within several decades of Boehme's death, most of his work was available in English, and it soon attracted the attention of the mystically inclined Cambridge Platonists, the Puritan poet John Milton, the scientist Isaac Newton, the Theosophists John Pordage and Jane Leade of the Philadelphian Society, and various groups among the religious radicals of the day, such as the Quakers. Later in England, Boehme's writings exerted a powerful influence on William Law and William Blake. On the continent, the German Pietists drank deep from the well of Boehme's wisdom, and both the Pietists and the Quakers exported Boehme to the North American continent. In the nineteenth century, German philosophers Friedrich Wilhelm von Schelling, Georg Wilhelm Friedrich Hegel, and Arthur Schopenhauer praised Boehme, and Samuel Taylor Coleridge was at one time an avid reader of Boehme. In the last century, Boehme clearly influenced the Jewish philosopher Martin Buber, the Protestant theologian Paul Tillich, the philosopher Martin Heidegger, the psychologist C. G. Jung, and the poet Robert Bly.

Boehme's Setting

Boehme lived from 1575 to 1624. His native city of Görlitz was in the province of Lusatia in the northern territory of the kingdom of Bohemia, which was ruled from Prague. The court of Rudolf II in Prague attracted thinkers engaged in many disciplines, inspired by a Renaissance spirit of humanism. Boehme's contemporaries included the philosopher René Descartes in France, the novelist Miguel de Cervantes in Spain, William Shakespeare in England, the early baroque composer Claudio Monteverdi in Italy, and the astronomer Johannes Kepler, who was in Prague in the early 1600s. It was an exciting intellectual era that saw the birth of new ideas in science and new forms in literature and music.

It was also an era of great conflict. The century preceding Boehme's birth had given rise to Protestantism, seen by its adherents as a powerful religious renewal. As often happens, however, renewal comes at the cost of division. Catholic and Protestant princes warred with one another in the name of religion. The final years of Jakob Boehme's life were shaped by the religious conflict of the Thirty Years' War (1618–1648), which ravaged central Europe. In addition to fighting Catholics on the battlefield, Protestants also fought among themselves in the pulpit. In Görlitz, as elsewhere, Lutherans and Calvinists collided over doctrine, and Boehme himself faced persecution from his own pastor for his unconventional theological ideas. These conflicts left Boehme convinced that the true task of religion is a spiritual transformation that seeks a faithful life at peace with others, rather than forces a confessional conformity through the use of violence.

Influences

Other influences were alive in Jakob Boehme's environment. In addition to Lutheran and Calvinist communities, there was an Anabaptist presence close to Görlitz. Anabaptists espoused a radical Christian discipleship. They insisted that church membership was a conscious adult choice that required the practice of church discipline. Anabaptists refrained from the use of the sword and the offices of magistracy that exercised violent means, and they demanded high moral standards from church members.

In and around Görlitz there was also a Schwenkfelder presence. Caspar Schwenckfeld (1490–1561) and his followers rejected Lutheran dogma and church hierarchy, preferring a spiritualized invisible church that was, as they saw it, free from hypocrisy. Schwenk-felders and Anabaptists endured in the face of persecution. Echoes of Schwenkfelder ideas are heard in Boehme's writings, particularly in his assertion that the true Christian community is a spiritual reality that is not identical with the "stone church" (*Steinkirche*) or the "walled church" (*Mauerkirche*).

Influential movements in Boehme's intellectual environment included astronomy, alchemy, and kabbalah. He lived in an age of tremendous change in scientific thought. His works reflect the transition from an earth-centered to a solar-centered universe, which suggests that he was in touch with wider currents in astronomy. His interest in the nature of the universe makes sense, since so much of his writing focuses on the story of Creation and its aftermath. Alchemy was still very much alive, and Boehme's contemporaries were acquainted with the thought of Paracelsus. For Boehme, alchemy was valuable because it held that the material world was imbued with spirit, and that inner transformation was the very purpose of life. Alchemy provided him with language to describe the new birth, the fundamental transformation toward perfection to which God invites the soul. The influences of kabbalah are more difficult to discern in Boehme, but it seems likely that the rich tradition of Jewish mysticism and its bold speculations concerning the inner workings of the Godhead offered him support as he reflected on the origins of evil. Like some of the Jewish mystics, Boehme does not hesitate to suggest that both good and evil find their roots in the divine.

Contours of His Thought

Although his writings exhibit an esoteric knowledge, for Boehme redemption is more about love and grace than it is about gnosis. The basic human problem is not insufficient knowledge, but rather a will that has gone astray. Salvation depends on a reorientation of the will by choosing to live in light and love.

Boehme's distinctive universe begins within the Godhead itself. Creation is out of God rather than out of nothing. But before the material world comes into being, there is within God's own self a process, though it takes place outside of time, within the realm of eternity. The primordial condition of the divine is as the *Ungrund*, the "unfathomed," sometimes translated as the "abyss." God is so simple, so unified, that God does not even have self-consciousness, since that would imply a division within the deity between the observer and that which is known. Within this unfathomed there arose a desire to know itself, and thus began the process of emanation of the Virgin Sophia, the figure of Wisdom from the book of Proverbs, who serves as an empty mirror in which the divine can perceive itself.

Boehme's universe is threefold. He speaks of three worlds: the world of darkness, fire, and wrath; the world of light, mercy, and love; and the visible world in which we humans find ourselves. Both the first and the second worlds are found in this third world, and it is in this third world that love and wrath, mercy and conflict, good and evil coexist—though not peacefully.

In the traditional Christian story, the Creation gives way to the Fall. In Boehme's understanding, Adam was created as a perfect being: androgynous, capable of reproduction without sexual organs, and without teeth or intestines, since he did not need to eat or digest in quite the same way as we do. In all these qualities he reflected divinity. Adam was intended to be espoused to Sophia. However, in his desire to satisfy his self-will, he abandoned God's will and the relationship with Sophia. When Adam lost Sophia, God created Eve as Adam's spouse so that Adam and Eve could live chastely in angelic bodies. They went on to eat the forbidden fruit, in conformity with the story in Genesis, but this was the last part of Adam's disobedience.

Redemption, the way to the restoration of the purity of Eden, is through spiritual regeneration or the new birth. Christ's incarnation and submission to the Father's will through death on the cross make salvation possible. However, this submission must be mirrored in each individual's yieldedness (*Gelassenheit*) to the divine will. To live in yieldedness is to renounce Adam's possessiveness and self-will, which opens the way out of wrath into the world of love. As already mentioned, both the world of wrath and the world of love are present in this third, visible world. It is the orientation of our own will that determines whether we inhabit the world of love by our yieldedness or the world of wrath by our selfishness. Boehme boldly states that both heaven and hell are present in this world. Both are to be found within it; they are interwoven but not visible to one another. In his understanding of the final state of all things at the end of time, Boehme blends traditional biblical imagery with his focus on the inwardness of spiritual reality and his hope for a restoration to the original state of Adam.

This is but the barest outline of the dense symbolic world of Jakob Boehme, a world that evolved over the years as he continued to think and to write. The complexity of his work may strike some readers as confusing, but it is our hope that the richness of the multilayered quality of his words will instead inspire a sense of wonderment that can open readers to experience the awe-inspiring reality that moved him to write.

Some Specific Topics

To understand the works of Boehme included in this volume, it may be helpful to consider some of his central ideas in greater detail: his notion of the seven characteristics of creation, the language of nature, the Virgin Sophia, and his alchemical-astrological angle of vision.

The Seven Characteristics

In his efforts to explain how the oneness of God can be the origin of the manifoldness of the created world, Boehme makes reference throughout his writings to a sevenfold system of characteristics or properties (*Eigenschaften*) that mediate between divine unity and natural multiplicity. These seven characteristics are central to his thought, and he describes them in almost endless variation, but there is a consistent pattern to his expositions of this concept. The first three characteristics are preanimate. The first one is a force of dryness, harshness, and contraction. The second is attraction, since for Boehme nature or creation begins in desire and expression, or "speaking forth." This second characteristic has a stinging, bitter quality. It is followed by the third characteristic, the capacity to perceive, which is a source of variety and differentiation, as well as anxiousness, in the natural world. These first three characteristics display the fierce quality of nature.

Then comes the fourth, the flash of fire that both looks back to the fierce properties and forward to life and love, which characterize the fifth property. The sixth characteristic is sound or tone. It is related to the capacity to understand, since sound enables language. The final characteristic is a summation, called variously body or enclosure, among others. It is a combination of the previous characteristics in an embodied nature.

It would be a mistake to understand this as a simple, straightforward process of unfolding from the first characteristic to the last. The seven properties intermingle in a playful love-wrestling in the light, as Boehme describes it. First one is uppermost, then another. Although nature may begin in fierceness, it concludes in a realm of joy and play.

Boehme offers a short summary of his teachings on these seven characteristics in his *Clavis*, a short work from 1624 intended as a "key" (which is the meaning of the Latin *clavis*) to his thought.

> Nature consists in its first foundation in seven characteristics, and the seven divide themselves further without limit.

> The first characteristic is desire, which makes dryness, sharpness, hardness, cold, and being.

The second characteristic is the movement or attraction of the desire. It makes stinging, breaking, and dividing of the hardness. It cuts up the attracted desire and brings it into multiplicity. It is a foundation of the bitter ache and is also the true root for life. It is the Vulcanus [an alchemical term for the power or governor of fire] for striking fire.

The third characteristic is the perceptibility in the breaking of the dry hardness. It is the foundation of anxiety and of the natural willing, in which the eternal will wishes to be revealed. That is, it wishes to be a fire or light, that is, a flash or radiance in which there appear the powers, colors, and virtues of being. In these three characteristics consist the basis of wrath and of hell and of all that is fierce.

The fourth characteristic is the fire, in which the oneness appears in the light, that is, in a love-fire, and the fierceness is the essence of the fire.

The fifth characteristic is the light with its love-power, in which the oneness in natural being collaborates.

The sixth characteristic is the sound or resonance, or the natural understanding, in which the five senses function spiritually, as in an intelligent life of nature.

The seventh characteristic is subject or enclosure of the other six characteristics, in which they function as life does in the flesh. The seventh is rightly called the foundation or the abode of nature, in which the characteristics stand in one ground.[3]

The Language of Nature

Sound is the sixth of Boehme's seven characteristics. The physical sounds in the bodily production of words fascinated him—the use of tongue, lips, and breath to make sounds that have meaning. He found support for his interest in words in his reading of the Bible. In the first chapter of Genesis, God called the universe into being through speech, in a series of commands beginning with "Let there be." Later, Adam assigned names to all the creatures. According to Boehme, Adam spoke the "language of nature," a language that reflected inward, innate qualities of creation. Boehme believed himself to be initiated into this primordial, superior language by divine inspiration. From his first book, *Aurora*, to his final major work, *The Great Mystery*, Boehme shows his interest in this language and offers interpretations of words in accordance with his notion of the language of nature. Often these explanations are a syllable-by-syllable dissection and re-creation of a word to determine its inner, secret meaning. Here is a sample from his book *The Threefold Life of Humankind*, which discusses the opening words of the Lord's Prayer, a prayer that "offers a very high and excellent understanding in the language of nature." Boehme discusses the first two phrases of the prayer, "Our Father in heaven, may your name be sanctified," which in his native German are *Unser Vater im Himmel, Dein Name werde geheiliget:*

> When we say "Our Father in heaven," the soul elevates itself in all three principles and appropriates that out of which the soul has been created. We understand this quite keenly and exactly in the language of nature. For *Un* is in the eternal will of God for nature. *Ser* contains within itself the first principle, in which the first forms of nature consist. *Vater* offers two distinctions of the two principles. For *Va* is the matrix on the cross. *Ter* is mercury in the center of nature. And they are two mothers in the eternal will, out of which all things have come to be, since the one separates itself into the fire and the other into the light of gentleness and into water. For *Va* is the mother from the light that gives being and *ter* is the mother of the transforming substance of fire that gives the great and strong life. And the *Vater* is both. When we say *im*, we understand what is within, that is, in the heart, from which the Spirit goes forth. For the syllable

im goes out of the heart and resounds through the lips, and the lips hold the heart unawakened within. When we say *Him*, we understand the creation of the soul. The syllable *mel* is the angelic soul itself, which the heart has grasped upon the cross between two mothers. And with the word *Him* a creature is created, that is, into *mel*. For *Him* is the dwelling of the *mel*. Therefore the soul is created in heaven, that is, in the matrix of love.

When we say *Dein*, we understand how the poor soul swims in the water of this world and throws itself with its will into the principle of God. For the soul goes by means of this syllable into the voice of God. In the syllable *Na*, the soul adapts itself, and in the syllable *me* the heavenly being grasps it. Thus this happens in the will of the soul. And when we say *wer*, then the whole creature goes into the will. For *wer* has the whole center. And with the syllable *de*, the soul lies down in obedience and in the gentleness, and does not wish to enkindle the *wer* in the fire, as Lucifer did. And when we say *ge*, the soul enters into heavenly being, as a silent child without anger. And the *hei* is the powerful entrance upon the cross in the Threeness, where the soul's will presses into the majesty in the light of God. With the syllable *li*, the soul's will has perceived the Holy Spirit. With *get*, the soul's will goes forth with the Holy Spirit. For the radiance of the majesty shines in the will, and the Holy Spirit enters in the radiance of the majesty upon the soul's coach. For the will is the soul's bridal coach, in which it enters into the Holy Threeness, in which the Holy Spirit sits with the radiance of the Godhead.[4]

Boehme's analysis can get even more microscopic than this. In chapter 4 of *Clavis*, he takes on the divine name *Jehova* letter by letter. The initial *J* (or *I*, since the two were often interchangeable at that time) is the "overflowing of the eternal inseparable unity, the sweet holiness of the foundation of divine I-ness." The *h* is the "word of breathing of the Threeness of God," while the *v* is the "joyful out-flowing of the breathing, that is, the forth-flowing Spirit of God." And on it goes.

In chapter 29 of his massive commentary on the book of Genesis, *The Great Mystery*, Boehme expounds on Adam's descendants as a "human tree" that has produced branches, twigs, and fruits out of its trunk—for evil and for good. The qualities of Adam's descendants are revealed in their names, as understood in the language of nature. Cain is a "source from the center of the fiery desire," which foreshadows his murderous character. Abel's "name in the language of nature means 'angel brought forth,'" signifying his innocence and his identity with the light-world rather than the fierce, fiery world of his brother. Boehme continues in this vein, showing how the characters of Mehujael and Methuselah are inherent in their very names, though Boehme refrains from a syllable-by-syllable analysis in that case.

And this seems to be the point of the language of nature for Boehme. Just as all the cosmos is bursting with divine meaning, the sounds of names also manifest this meaning because they reflect the primal, divine utterance that brought everything into being.

The Virgin Sophia, Divine Wisdom

The concept of an androgynous God with female and male aspects in perfect balance is a remarkable notion found in Boehme's writings. Boehme personified this female aspect as Sophia, the Greek name for "wisdom." He drew on wisdom traditions in the Hebrew Bible, particularly Proverbs, in shaping his concept of Sophia. Although the concept was by no means new in either Jewish or Christian speculative thought, Boehme developed the idea in his own distinctive way. His work influenced generations of later German writers, particularly among the Radical Pietists in the seventeenth and eighteenth centuries.

Boehme did not present Sophia as a fourth person of the Trinity, despite accusations to that effect even in his own time. He was consistently Trinitarian in his theology—therefore he regards Sophia neither as a separate deity apart from the Godhead nor as a divine spouse of God. Certain other writers identify her as an alternative personification of the Holy Spirit or as a figure symbolizing the church; for Boehme, however, Sophia is the personification of the female aspect of God. This idea is central to Boehme's notion that God possesses both female and male characteristics. In this regard, Boehme departs quite strikingly from the theological legacy of the Protestant Reformation of the sixteenth century.

Sophia, according to Boehme, was always a part of the Godhead. As Boehme conceived of God possessing both love and wrath, characterized as light and fire, he assigned the loving and merciful part of God to the female aspect, Sophia. This function was also assigned to Jesus Christ.

In Boehme's view of the Creation, Adam was created androgynous, hence fully in the image of God. Adam possessed both male and female characteristics in perfect balance. Boehme tended to write of this balance using the metaphor of marriage, personifying Sophia as a spouse to Adam. When Adam desired to follow his own will, rather than rely completely on God's will, Adam fell into sin. This sin broke the balance and unity of female and male aspects within Adam. The female aspect of Adam, personified as Sophia, disappeared. Using the metaphor of marriage for gender balance, Boehme wrote that Adam lost Sophia as his spouse, and Adam's gender aspects were divided as a result of this breaking of his unified will. The female aspect of humanity was then embodied in Eve, the first woman.

In Boehme's works, Sophia's relationship to Jesus Christ is complex. She does not replace Jesus as the revealer of God's love and mercy. Jesus, the Son of God in Boehme's theology, reveals and embodies the love that is always a part of God the Father. Jesus's death on the cross and his resurrection are the ultimate act of salvation to redeem humanity from sin, wrath, and the human inclination to dominate people, which Boehme tended to see as a male characteristic. Yet Sophia is very much present in Jesus's ministry, and particularly in his death on the cross. Upon Christ's death, which he undertook out of love for sinners, Sophia is united with Christ in a way that opens the possibility of restoration of the union of female and male aspects in humanity, which occurs through spiritual rebirth. Thus Sophia becomes a coagent for spiritual rebirth in union with Christ.

As the personification of God's female aspect, Sophia draws people into a relationship of love and faith with God. Boehme describes her as wooing believers, drawing them into a tender relationship of love for God. At the same time, she can be forceful, directing the relationship and even chastising those who become unfaithful. This directive dimension of Sophia tends to be an effort to draw people back from waywardness into a single-hearted love for God.

In her role with Christ as giver of rebirth, she is a kind of mother figure in Boehme's multivalent account of the spiritual life. At the same time, she bids believers to love God and remain faithful. Thus she serves also as a kind of spouse figure for the soul. In these ways, the feminine aspect of God and God's activity is present in God's eternal existence, in creation, in salvation, and in the restoration of humanity to the image of God through spiritual rebirth.

Boehme offers some reflections on Sophia in the following excerpt from his lengthy work *The Threefold Life of Humankind*:

> This Wisdom of God is an eternal virgin, not a wife but rather chastity and purity without flaw, who stands as an image of God. She is a likeness of the Threeness. She gives birth to nothing, but rather in her stand the great miracles that the Holy Spirit beholds, and that the word of the Father creates through the dry matrix, that is, through the creative command, and she is the wisdom of miracles without number. In her the Holy Spirit beholds the image of

the angels, as well as the image of human beings that the creative word has created.

She is the great mystery in the counsel of God, and she enters into the second principle, which in the original condition is the first, that is, the wrath of the Father, and she reveals the miracles of the hidden seals or forms of nature in the fierceness. And she is apprehended by nothing, for she is an image of birthing but has no being. Through her the Holy Spirit has beheld the third principle, that is, this world, which the creative word has created corporeally out of both matrices of substance. To this being the Holy Spirit has beheld a goal in the center with her bodily being, but both mothers are to stand in the substance, before the Virgin of Wisdom, before the Threeness in the eternal figure, to the wonder and glory of God.

Therefore concern yourselves, you philosophers: how God has created this world in six days. For the work of each day is a creation of a spirit in the Holy Threeness, and the seventh day is the rest of the Sabbath of God, in the seventh spirit of God, where the Virgin of Wisdom stands within. There is no more working of anxiety but rather the eternal perfection of rest.

For the six spirits must pour out the works that are in their seals and were not known before, until they have poured out the bowls of their power in the principle of this world, to bring the human creatures into being and deeds, like an edifice to God's eternal deeds of wonder.

And when this is accomplished, then the hidden spirits of God return under the seals into the ether, that is, into their center, and the time of the seventh seal in the realm of God begins, as the book of Revelation of Jesus Christ attests and as we have known in the Holy Threeness.

This Wisdom of God, which is a virgin of gracefulness and a likeness of the Threeness, is in its figure an image like angels and human beings, and takes its origin in the center on the cross, that is, a flower of the plant from the Spirit of God.

For she is the substance of the Spirit, which the Spirit of God leads into itself as a garment in which the Holy Spirit reveals itself; otherwise the Holy Spirit's form would not be known. For she is the Spirit's corporeality, and although she is not a corporeal, perceptible being like us humans, she is yet real and visible.

For we humans can see nothing more of God's Spirit in eternity than the radiance of its majesty, and we feel God's glorious power in us, for this power is our life and leads us.

But we recognize the virgin in all heavenly images. Although she gives the body to all fruits, she is not the corporeality of the fruits but rather the gracefulness and beauty in them.[5]

Alchemy and Astrology

In Boehme's time, the discipline of empirical investigation of natural phenomena had not yet fully emerged. What would become the science of chemistry was indistinguishable from alchemy, just as astronomy was from astrology. Most people in the West still believed that faith in God could unlock understanding of the visible world around them. Conversely, they believed that interpreting the natural world correctly would help them to understand God better. The visible world was full of spiritual significance. Those who could "read" the signs of the spiritual world could gain insights into God's designs. For many people, everything had some spiritual significance. A comet, a spark, a fire, or a plant might all reveal something about God's intentions for good or for judgment and punishment. Some speculative thinkers and mystics sought a way to make spiritual connections and find meaning in all phenomena, from distant stars to precious and common metals, from plants to planets. This search for a knowledge and spirituality that were all interconnected inspired Boehme's quest during a time when the Protestant Reformation had unraveled past unities of the Christian faith in Europe.

For Boehme, the known planets numbered six: Mercury, Venus, Earth, Mars, Jupiter, and Saturn, along with the sun and the moon. Boehme accepted the new discovery—still considered heresy—that the sun was the center of the solar system, not a body revolving around the Earth. Each of the planets had a corresponding spiritual significance, and each had a corresponding metal. Just as the planets and constellations could work good or ill on people, so the metals and substances of the earth could signify spiritual processes in their reactions with each other.

Boehme embraced the medieval legacy of alchemy, which was derived from even older traditions. He inherited the ancient view that the cosmos was composed of four elements, namely, earth, fire, air, and water. In addition he worked within the framework that was common up until the early modern period and promoted by the great alchemist Paracelsus, which claimed that all external material was based in some way on the foundational elements of salt, sulfur, and mercury.

Working with the inherited traditions of associating spiritual truths with attempts to separate precious metals from base materials, Boehme gave his unique imprint to the spiritual significance of alchemy. Thus his frequent theme of spiritual rebirth could be distilled from various strategies for treating lead or other coarse substances in order to find gold or other precious metals. For Boehme, the love of Jesus Christ that forgives sinners was the external substance that could transform them into spiritually reborn children of God, in a kind of spiritual transmutation. The resulting spiritual rebirth removes the coarse, damaging effects of sin, and renders the sinner a precious child of God. Christ's love is like the transforming substance applied to base materials in order to generate precious metals. The trials of renouncing sin or adversity from others are similar in Boehme's view to the various processes an alchemist might use on base materials to separate or refine valuable metals from them.

One alchemical term that Boehme frequently used is particularly rich in connotation: the archaic word "tincture." Originally the term meant "dyed" or "colored," and it is related to the modern words "tinged" and "tinted." In modern pharmaceutical usage, a tincture is a medicinal substance in a solution of alcohol—readers may be acquainted with the expression "tincture of iodine," for example. In the early modern chemistry of Boehme's contemporaries, a tincture was the "essential principle" of a given substance, contained in solution, whereas in alchemy a tincture was an immaterial substance whose character could be communicated to or infused into material substances. An alchemical tincture was therefore an agent of transformation, an essence that imparted its qualities to the object into which it was introduced. Fire and light, for example, act as a tincture on water and make it into blood. Spiritually, the blood of Christ is a tincture that transforms people from captivity in the realm of wrath to the freedom and joy of the realm of light and love. Because the term "tincture" is obscure, in this translation we have used the expression "transforming substance" to convey this key concept.

While Boehme's use of astrology and alchemy are much more detailed and complicated than this simple introduction can describe, for him they both served first and foremost as linguistic tools for expressing spiritual truth. His confidence that astrology and alchemy in a Christian context could also explain all knowledge of natural phenomena remained as strong as his belief that rightly understanding the stars and the elements (as he knew them) would direct people to God.

Some of Boehme's most strongly alchemical language occurs in passages of *The Signature of All Things* (*De signatura rerum*). He summarized all of the alchemical elaborations in chapter 5, saying that the "entire work" consists of "two things, a heavenly and an earthly: the heavenly should make within itself the earthly into a heavenly thing, and eternity should make time in itself into eternity."

More detailed and obtuse usage of alchemical and astrological language appears in the short passage from the third chapter of *The Signature of All Things* offered below. Boehme described all things— the sun, stars, elements, and all creatures—as being a revelation of eternity. All things must undergo a separation through a fiery process, which is compared to a flash of lightning that has both fire and light. Boehme's expression "sal nitric flash" likely refers to the explosive quality of potassium nitrate, the active ingredient in gunpowder, which fascinated alchemists in his day. Like other alchemical processes, this flash becomes a symbol for spiritual realities. The process of separation will reveal spiritual characteristics, just as an alchemical separation reveals the characteristics of coarse or precious materials. Just as such a separation draws valuable materials from the various mixings of salt, sulfur, and mercury in the material world, the separation of self-will from the desire to submit freely to God's will reveals the most precious spiritual life, which is comparable to gold:

> After the creation of the high spirits, God created this visible world with stars and elements, as a birth out of the eternal mother of all being, so that everything proceeded from the eternal beginning, and had a temporal beginning. For here we should consider, that the eternal bearer moved herself, and enkindled her form, so that the one became bodily in the other. But afterward God created the earth. Therefore we should consider the following:
>
> The first desire toward nature pressed itself and led itself with the impression in three forms, that is, sulfur, mercury, and salt. And everything in the impression became weighty and moveable, which is not the case in the silent nothing; and everything drives itself to the highest anxiety, up to the sal nitric flash, which is the cause of fire. Thus the torment goes whirling in itself, like the boiling of water because of fire. For the strong desire draws toward itself, and that which is fiery, which is in sulfur, presses out.

Thus the astringent drawing is a fierce sting, that is, a shattering, and yet this fierce sting is maintained by the astringency, so that it cannot withdraw. Thus it is and becomes painful, just as a turning or boiling, which yet is only spirit without being. This happens in mercury, and is the form of mercury itself. There is the separating of two kinds of wills, such that one remains, and is the same anxious being, namely that which arises from desire. The other, which is from the pleasure of freedom, and yet is not a separation or withdrawing from one another, and thus goes with each other through the fire's kindling through the sal nitric flash. There occurs the dying in fierceness of the fire, at the fire's kindling, because the torment dies, and yet it is no death. Rather, it is a likeness of death, and yet is thus the true, eternal, and temporal death.

Here freedom grasps itself, and death or the flash falls powerless into freedom and releases itself. Thus the spirit, namely the quality, becomes material (that is to say, the very sharp, fiery quality of dread) and it retains only an essential working, like a powerless desire. In the igniting of the fire in the sal nitric flash, each characteristic separates within itself, and the entire material becomes a particular thing, namely, metal, stone, and earth.

The highest metal, namely gold, originates from freedom, which is grasped by the flash in the astringent impressing. However, it is not free from other material, for it is grasped by everything simultaneously. But because freedom is grasped by the *sul* or characteristic of light,[6] the *sul* presses outward for the revelation of itself, as the characteristic of pleasure is freed. For this reason metals grow, but the coarse, hard stones do not, because they are grasped too hard by the impression that comes from the fierce being, and they have too little *sul* in themselves. Concerning precious stones, however, with their gleam and great value, they have their origin in the lightning of fire, in which death separates from life. Because a portion within them goes beneath itself because of the dark being, and the other portion goes above itself because of freedom, and yet in the flash everything leads itself into being, so the same flash becomes material. Therefore gems are hard and sparkling like an eye, for this is also the origin of the eye or shining in the body, when life is kindled, all according to the rule of eternity. And therefore there is so much power and virtue, because they stand so close to deity and bear the embodied name of divine power. Just as gold is close to the divine or heavenly being, so one may dissolve the body that has died and make it into a flowing, soaring spirit, which can happen only through God's moving. One would see what this becomes, which no reason believes or understands without divine seeing.

We should also consider further the other metals and minerals, which also have their origin thus. However, in the sal nitric flash each characteristic separates itself, for we see that the characteristic of the fire and the light are different, and all of this is from the first impression. For before the impression of freedom, pleasure and desire are within each other. Similarly, chaos is within the view of great wonders, in which all colors, powers, and virtues lie within this single chaos or eye of wonders. God is this chaos, that is, the Being of All Beings, who is revealed in that which is particular with the eye of eternity. Each material is a being according to the spirit from which it is born. If one kindles the material in fire, it will also give off a light according to the spirit in the being.

Therefore we should also consider the metals, and what kind of spirit is in each one, also what kind of gleam it has, and also its body. Just as the will swings the senses from the highest to the lowest, and the lowest to the highest is grasped by the senses, therefore the eternal mind is revealed from the highest majesty into the lowliest part, that is, into the greatest darkness. This world, with sun, stars, and elements, together with every creaturely being, is nothing other than a revelation of eternity, of the eternal will and mind. As it was in the beginning, thus it is still in its boiling and growing, thus driving on to light and darkness, to good and evil. Everything is in these first three forms, namely, sulfur, mercury, and salt, each in one degree after another.[7]

Boehme's Style

Boehme's sentences tend to be lengthy constructions with numerous relative clauses, as was typical of the European prose of his age. To a modern reader, the relationship of these clauses to one another yields itself only after repeated readings. To make things easier for the reader, we have shortened many of these sentences, and in places we have supplied words that we feel reveal the nature of one clause's relationship to another as temporal, causal, concessive, consequential, and the like.

A peculiar feature of Boehme's style is his use of the relative conjunction *als* to string together a long sentence. In his day, *als* could mean "as," "when," or "therefore," and at times even "in as much as," "so," "thus," or "because." Very often, however, he means simply "namely" or "that is." After encountering a great many of these, one may get the impression that Boehme is just thinking aloud, writing appositive expressions as they come to him. It seems possible that perhaps he wrote, at least at times, in order to experience the insights that came to him in the act of writing itself. This may help us to understand why Boehme wrote so much—thousands of pages, mostly during the last five years of his life. Most of his texts focus on the same cluster of themes, particularly human and cosmic origins, the human departure from this pristine state, and the possibility of return and restoration through the new birth. He returned constantly to these themes of creation, fall, and redemption, always endeavoring to clarify his understanding. It seems likely he anticipated that the act of reading could be for the reader what the act of writing was for him: an experience of ever-increasing insight and clarity. While a contemporary reader might find Boehme's endless strings of appositional phrases initially tedious, we recommend that you read them slowly and generously. Try to encounter each "that is" as a new angle by which to consider what precedes it, or as an unfolding of what is inherent in the words that come before. Otherwise you may be tempted to hear each "namely" as merely a seventeenth-century equivalent of a filler word in popular contemporary speech patterns, such as the word "like" in informal conversation. Hearing *als* as "like" will not open the reader to the gradual exfoliation of Jakob Boehme's thought, which his use of the word *als* serves.

Texts Chosen for This Volume

The texts selected for inclusion in this volume represent Boehme's work but do not exhaust his thought, which developed over the years even as it remained constant in terms of his larger interests. Toward the end of his life, Boehme penned some shorter essays that summarize many of the ideas expressed in his lengthy works. We have chosen three of these treatises that represent his mature thought: *Life Beyond the Senses*, *The New Birth*, and *True Yieldedness*. These are followed by some selections from *The Incarnation of Jesus Christ*, where Boehme's reflections on rebirth and redemption show his engagement with these great themes of Christian theology. Finally, there is Boehme's treatise *Six Mystical Points*, a relatively short but quite dense essay.

It is our hope that, having experienced this taste of Jakob Boehme, readers will feel both eager and prepared to explore more of his rich body of work on their own.[8]

A Note on Scripture

Boehme's use of the Bible is frequent and familiar, sometimes almost to the point of being casual. At times he quotes the Bible directly, at other times he refers to it, and at still other times he paraphrases it slightly. Even when he quotes directly, he of course uses the translation that was commonly used in his era and in his language, namely that of the great Protestant reformer Martin Luther. Luther sometimes translated the original Hebrew or Greek in a way somewhat different from what readers of the Bible in English are accustomed to. In light of all this, we have chosen simply to translate Boehme's words directly, supplying (as he often does himself) a reference to the original scriptural source. Readers who have an acquaintance with the Bible should be forewarned that in Boehme's works they will encounter slight variations of familiar biblical passages.

A Note on the Translation

For centuries it has been the practice in the German language to capitalize all nouns. This can pose a challenge for translators: often in religious texts translators tend to espouse at least a bit of theology by capitalization—for example, to write "Spirit" when the noun obviously refers to God, but "spirit" when it refers to another being, such as a human spirit or one of Boehme's seven source-spirits. Since all appearances of the word for "spirit" (*Geist*) in Boehme's writings are capitalized, translators have to decide whose spirit Boehme is referring to. Similarly, at times the "word of God" simply means a divine utterance, while at other times the phrase is a reference to Christ, who, in the opening verses of the Gospel according to John, is called the Word of God. Likewise it seems appropriate to capitalize the word for "wisdom" when the word unambiguously refers to the Virgin Sophia. In cases that were less clear, we have left "wisdom" lowercase. It is possible that Boehme, who often prefers to work by poetic suggestion rather than direct assertion, wants his readers to hear at least a faint echo of the Virgin Sophia in almost every occurrence of the word "wisdom." By choosing to leave such words and phrases without capitalization, we invite readers to enter imaginatively into the world of Boehme's thought and to decide for themselves what they think Boehme's intentions were.

In previous printed editions of Boehme's texts, it has been the custom to number each paragraph. These numbers make for easy reference to his writings, but they seemed to pose an obstacle for new readers of Boehme, so they have been omitted in this book. To help newcomers navigate their way through Boehme's thoughts, which at times resemble a meandering stroll through the forest rather than a focused march on a straight path, we have added occasional subheadings for smoother reading.

Words of Encouragement to Readers

Reading Jakob Boehme is both an adventure and a challenge. He didn't expect us to get it all, but he did expect us to get something, or as he put it, "Not everyone will understand my writings according to my meaning, indeed not anyone. But each receives according to his or her gift, to his or her betterment, one more than the other, according as the Spirit has its characteristic in him or her."[9]

Boehme concedes that his writings are difficult to grasp. This could cause frustration for a reader—or even despair for his translators!—but that need not be so. Instead, it can become an invitation to be Boehme's collaborator in exploring the fundamental questions of life. His words are an invitation to ponder and to puzzle, but they are also an invitation to awe and wonder.

His works seek to describe an experience that is beyond the peripheral vision of ordinary rational thought, so he is constantly pushing language to its limits. Furthermore, he not only invites his readers to an inward synthesis, but he is himself trying to model a synthesis of various ideas and modes of thought in his writings. As a result, his writings blend together several language worlds: biblical, theological, alchemical, astrological, and others. Like the polyphonic music of his contemporaries, his writings are a contrapuntal interplay of voices. Even as his words reveal something new, they also veil something, so that readers might feel compelled to step into this complex idea-world and experience additional meanings for themselves. In other words, Boehme's goal is not simply to describe spiritual transformation, but also to encourage the reader—even if at times this encouragement feels more like cajoling—to embrace that transformation.

LIFE BEYOND THE SENSES

JAKOB BOEHME wrote *Life Beyond the Senses* in 1622. It was first published with several other essays in a volume entitled *The Way to Christ*. The piece is composed as a dialogue, or more precisely a series of questions and answers, between a student and a spiritual teacher. In this rhetorical frame, Boehme invites the reader to identify with the spiritual seeker and to embrace the inner realities that the teacher offers. *Life Beyond the Senses* offers both a spiritual method and an introduction to many of Boehme's central theological ideas. It is therefore a good place to begin an exploration of the rich inner world of Jakob Boehme.

Many of Boehme's works are filled with imagery and encourage the use of the imagination as a spiritual practice. Contrasting yet complementary practices aim to achieve an emptiness or imageless-ness of mind by abstaining from the use of mental activities such as thought, imagination, and feeling. In *Life Beyond the Senses* we see the imageless dimension of Boehme's spirituality. The reader is admonished to "swing yourself up for a moment into that in which no creature dwells," and to "remain silent from all of your willing and sensing" in order to experience God directly. As Boehme boldly states, "You are what God was before nature and creatureliness."

Boehme's metaphors are bidirectional. In addition to swinging up like an arc heavenward, he also tells his reader to sink down "into the ground of God's mercy." Whether the motion is upward or downward, the goal is to leave the world behind, in order to "come into that from which the world was made."

Here Boehme participates in a long tradition of Christian spiritual practices that aspire to imagelessness. Like his spiritual forebears, he holds that such a practice is safe. Our imaginations can deceive us, and the forces of evil can do the same by introducing images into our consciousness that lead us astray. As Boehme puts it, the devil can place false desires in us. These are in conflict with God's will. This is crucial for Boehme because the basic human problem, as he sees it, is that people do not want what God wants. It is the human will that is the difficulty. So while he advocates an imageless practice, it is not because our capacity to think or to imagine is the problem. Rather, because images can evoke desires, and because it is our will that chooses whether or not to act on a desire, he advocates forsaking all sensing and willing. As he suggests, love is crowded out by the false desires that take root in the imagination.

To sink into God, to become as nothing, is to yield to selfless love. "Yieldedness" (Gelassenheit) is a word in the German mystical tradition that also connotes equanimity, inner calm, and serenity. Later in this volume readers will find an entire treatise devoted to this concept. Here we should note that yielding is an act of will. It is a spiritual method that is based on the understanding that the will determines the orientation of the soul. To contemporary ears, the act of yielding may sound only negative, but the practice leads to fulfillment, not to self-destruction. The result of yielding oneself to the will of God is an experience of divine love, joy, and a playfulness that is heavenly.

In fact, for Boehme, heaven and hell are found within. Both are present in this world, and as a consequence of the exercise of the will, a person lives in love or in wrath. Central to Boehme's understanding of the cosmos and its essential unity is that all three worlds—the fire-world of wrath, the light-world of love, and the present earthly world—mutually dwell in one another. Therefore heaven and hell are each in the other, but "as a nothing," and so neither is aware of the presence of the other.

The discussion of the internal heaven leads the student to ask about the final condition of all things. In Christian terms, this includes the resurrection of the dead and the Last Judgment. The teacher replies that each soul is judged at death, but on the last day there will be a separation of good and evil. In a rather unusual interpretation of the final resurrection, Boehme explains that the resurrected body will be material, but it will be crystalline rather than the coarse, bestial stuff that resulted from the Fall. These transparent bodies will have spiritual flesh and blood—a concept that is important to Boehme's understanding of the nature of Christ, of redemption, and of the "testaments," as he refers to the Christian sacraments. (He develops these ideas more fully in his work *The Incarnation of Jesus Christ*, which is excerpted in a later chapter in this book.) In that final state, all will be simply one in Christ, like a tree with its branches. This point is so important to Boehme that he repeats it in this essay. All people will be of one gender, "male virgins" (note here that the German word for virgin is *Jungfrau*, literally "young woman," so the word always carries a feminine connotation). In other works included in this volume, Boehme develops his concept of Adam as originally androgynous. Sexual differentiation is a consequence of the Fall in Eden. In that final state in heaven, there will be no more possessiveness, and life will be characterized by joy and play. Hell will continue in the location of this world, but it will be hidden to heaven.

In the meantime, that sinful possessiveness continues to dominate life in this world, and human society is characterized by injustice, as well as oppression of the poor, the disempowered, and genuine Christians. Boehme is more than a speculative philosopher. He is concerned with everyday ethics and their cosmic consequences. Like the biblical prophets, he has a profound concern for social justice for the oppressed. The root of oppression is self-centeredness—this is the practical application of his philosophical speculations on love and wrath. In strong words, Boehme condemns the violence and injustice of those "who torment the poor and wretched and suck the sweat out of them, oppress them, and drag them off by force, and regard them as trash underfoot." Driven by false desires, earthly rulers wage wars for ostensibly religious purposes. In another work, *The Great Mystery*, he echoes these protests against war.[1]

> For all war that the Christians wage is the sword of the cherub and Babel. The true Christians wage no war, for they have shattered the cherub's sword in Christ's death and have died in Christ and risen in him, and no longer live to outward might and dominion, for their realm is revealed in Christ and is not of this world.[2]

The future state of love and bliss are so inviting. Why, asks the student, is there such conflict now? Boehme responds that pain and strife reveal the joy. Knowledge relies on distinctions. In the primordial unity, Adam did not know good and evil. Pain—and here it is useful to recall that Boehme wrote amid the horrors of the Thirty Years' War, a conflict begun allegedly on religious grounds—manifests its opposite, joy.

The student said to the teacher, "How may I come to that life beyond the senses that I may see God and hear God speak?" The teacher said, "If you can swing yourself up for a moment into that in which no creature dwells, then you will hear what God speaks."

The student said, "Is that near or far?" The teacher said, "It is within you. If you could remain silent from all of your willing and sensing for one hour, then you will hear unutterable words of God."

The student said, "How may I hear when I keep silent from sensing and willing?" The teacher said, "If you keep silent from sensing and willing of your self, then the eternal hearing, seeing, and speaking will be revealed within you, and God will hear and see through you. Your own hearing, willing, and seeing hinder you, so that you do not see or hear God."

The student spoke, "With what shall I hear and see God, if God is beyond nature and creaturely life?" The teacher spoke, "If you would remain silent, then you are what God was before nature and creatureliness, that from which God created your nature and creatureliness. So hear and see with what God saw and heard in you, before your own willing, seeing, and hearing began."

The Problem of Selfish Willing

The student spoke, "What then hinders me from coming to this?" The teacher spoke, "Your own willing, hearing, and seeing, and the fact that you strive against that from which you have come. With your own willing, you separate your self from God's willing. With your own seeing, you see only into your own willing. And your willing blocks your hearing with a self-sensing of earthly, natural things. They lead you into a ground, and overshadow you with what you want. Consequently you may not come to that which is beyond the natural and beyond the senses."

The student spoke, "If I stand in nature, how can I come through nature into the ground beyond the senses, without a shattering of nature?" The teacher answered, "Three things pertain to this. The first thing is that you give over your will to God, and sink into the ground of God's mercy. The second thing is that you hate your own willing, and do not do what your will drives you to do. The third thing is that you subjugate yourself in patience to the cross of our Lord Jesus Christ, that you may bear the afflictions of nature and creatureliness. If you do this, God will speak into you, and will lead your yielded will into God's self, into the ground beyond nature, and then you will hear what the Lord speaks within you."

Letting Go of the Creaturely

The student spoke, "So must I forsake the world and my life, if I am to do this?" The teacher spoke, "If you forsake the world, you will come into that from which the world was made. And if you lose your life, and come into the powerlessness of your ability, your life will stand in God, for whose sake you forsook your life, and from whom your life came forth into a body."

The student spoke, "God created the human in the natural life, that the human should rule over all creatures on earth, and be a ruler over all life in this world. Therefore the human must possess it all as property." The teacher spoke, "If it is the case that you rule only outwardly over all creatures, then in your willing and ruling you are in a bestial demeanor. You stand only in a figurative, transitory ruling. Also, you are leading your desire into a bestial essence, by which you will be infected and imprisoned, and will receive a bestial demeanor. However, if it is the case that you have forsaken the figurative orientation, then you stand in that which is beyond the figurative. You rule in the ground above all creatures, from which they were created, and nothing on earth may harm you, for you are equal to all things, and nothing is unequal to you."[3]

The student spoke, "Oh dear teacher, teach me how I may come the closest to this, that I am equal to all things." The teacher spoke, "Gladly. Think about the words of our Lord Jesus Christ, when he spoke, 'Unless you turn and become like children, you will not see the realm of God' (Matt. 18:3). If it is the case now that you want to be equal to all things, then you must forsake all things, and turn your desire away from them, and do not desire them, nor presume for yourself to own any thing as a possession. For as soon as you have grasped a something in your desire, and allow it in yourself and take possession of it, then that something becomes a concrete thing in you. It works on your will, so that you are obligated to protect that thing, and relate to it as though it were your own being. But if you take nothing into your desire, then you are free of all things and at the same time you rule over all things. For you have nothing in your receptivity, and you are a nothing to all things, and all things are to you as nothing. You are like a child, who does not understand what a thing is. And if you do understand it, you understand it without its disturbing your perceiving, in a manner like that in which God rules all things, and sees [all things], and yet no thing grasps God. But because you said that I should teach you how you may come to this, then look at the words of Christ, who said, 'Without me you can do nothing' (John 15:5). In your own capability you cannot come to such a rest that no creature disturbs you, unless you give yourself over completely to the life of our Lord Jesus Christ, and give over your willing and desire completely to Christ, and will nothing without Christ. So if you stand with your body in the world and its characteristics, and with your reason under the cross of our Lord Christ, but with your will you walk in heaven, and stand at the end point from which all creatures have come and to which they will go again, then you may look on everything outwardly with your reason, and inwardly with your soul's mind and with Christ, to whom all power is given in heaven and on earth, to rule in and over all things" (Matt. 28:18).[4]

The student spoke, "Oh teacher, the creatures that live within me hold me, so that I cannot completely give up myself, no matter how much I want to do so." The teacher said, "If your will goes out from the creatures, then the creatures are forsaken in you and they are in the world, and only your body is with the creatures, while you walk spiritually with God. And if your will forsakes the creatures, then the creatures have died in your will, and they live only in the body in the world. And so if your will is not introduced into the creatures, they cannot disturb the soul. For St. Paul says, 'Our life is in heaven' (Phil. 3:20). Again: 'You are the temple of the Holy Spirit, who lives in you' (1 Cor. 6:19). So the Holy Spirit lives in the will, and the creatures live in the body."

The student spoke, "If the Holy Spirit lives in the will of the soul's mind, how may I be certain that the Spirit will not fade away from me?" The teacher spoke, "Listen to the words of our Lord Jesus Christ, who said, 'If you remain in my word, then my words will remain in you.'⁵ If it is the case that you remain with your will in the words of Christ, then his word and Spirit remain in you. But if it is the case that your will goes into creatures, you have broken yourself away from him and you can no longer be certain, unless you remain constantly in yielded humility, and you give yourself to continual repentance, so that you always have remorse that creatures live in you. If you do that, then you remain according to the will in a daily dying to the creatures, and in a daily ascension to heaven."

Repentance

The student spoke, "Oh dear teacher, teach me how I may always come into continual repentance." The teacher spoke, "If you forsake that which loves you, and you love that which hates you, then you will stand constantly in repentance."

The student spoke, "What is that?" The teacher spoke, "Your creatures in flesh and blood, as well as all those people who love them that love you, because your will cares for all these people. The will must forsake all of them and consider them enemies. And you hate the cross of our Lord Jesus Christ, along with the ridicule of the world. You must learn to love the cross and the world's ridicule and take them up for daily practice of your repentance. Then you will have constant cause to hate yourself with the creatures, and to seek the eternal rest in which your will may rest. As Christ said, 'In me you have rest, but in the world you have anguish.'"[6]

Swing to Where No Creature Is

The student spoke, "How may I recover from such afflictions?" The teacher spoke, "If at all hours you swing away from all creatures, above all sensory reason, into the most pure mercy of God, into the suffering of our Lord Jesus Christ, and give yourself over to it, so you will receive strength to rule over sin, death, the devil, hell, and the world, so you will withstand all assaults."

The student spoke, "How can it occur for me, a poor human, so that with the soul's mind I may attain that condition where no creature is?" The teacher spoke quite kindly to him, "Oh dear student, if only it were the case that your will might break off from all creatureliness for just one hour, and could swing to that place where no creature is. Then your will would be clothed with the greatest radiance of the glory of God. Your will would taste the sweetest love of our Lord Jesus Christ, which no person can utter, and would sense within yourself the unutterable words of our Lord Jesus Christ, from his great mercy.[7] The will would feel in itself that the cross of our Lord Christ was transformed into a tender beneficence. The will would then rather win this cross than any of the world's honor and good."

The student said, "How then would it be for the body, since it must live in creatureliness?" The teacher spoke, "The body would be placed in the discipleship of our Lord Christ, who said that his realm is not of this world. It would commence to die outwardly and inwardly. Outwardly it would die to the vanity of the world and evil deeds, and would become opposed to and inimical to all haughtiness. Inwardly it would be opposed to all evil longing and inclination, and receive a thoroughly new sense and will, which is constantly directed toward God."

The World Outside,
a New World Within

The student spoke, "The world would therefore hate and despise such a person, because this person must contradict the world, and live and do otherwise than the world." The teacher spoke, "Such a person would not take this as a sorrow. Rather the person would rejoice that the person has become worthy to resemble the image of our Lord Christ, and would want to bear gladly the cross of our Lord, so that only Christ's sweetest love infuses the person."[8]

The student spoke, "How would it be with that person, if the wrath of God inwardly and the evil world outwardly would attack that one, as happened to our Lord Christ?" The teacher spoke, "It would be for that one as it was for our Lord Christ. When he was insulted by the world and the priests, and was crucified, he commended his soul into the hands of the Father, and departed from the anguish of this world into eternal joy. Therefore such a person would penetrate into the great love of God within, away from all mockery and anguish of the world, and would be made alive and upheld, preserved through the sweetest name of Jesus. The person would see and sense a new world within, which penetrates beyond God's wrath. In this new world the person would wrap the soul with equanimity, and regard everything with such, whether the body be in hell or on earth. The soul's mind of that person would certainly be in the great love of God."

The student spoke, "But how would one's body be nourished in the world, and how would one nourish one's own, if all the disfavor of the world fell upon one?" The teacher spoke, "One receives a greater favor than the world can bestow, because one has God and all angels as one's friends who protect one in all distress, therefore also God is one's blessing in all things. And even if things should occur differently than God would want, it is only a test and an attraction of love, so that the person should pray to God even more, and commend all one's ways to God."

Good Friends Endure

The student said, "But one will lose all good friends, and no one will stand by this person in distress." The teacher spoke, "One receives the heart of all good friends as a possession, and loses only enemies, who beforehand had loved the person's vanity and wickedness."

The student said, "How does that happen, that one receives good friends as a possession?" The teacher said, "One receives as brothers and sisters of one's own life all the souls who belong to our Lord Jesus. For God's children are but one in Christ, and Christ is in all. Therefore one receives them all as bodily members in Christ. For they have the heavenly goods all in common, and live in one love of God, like the branches of a tree from one sap. Further, just like our Lord Christ, they cannot lack outward, natural friends. The high priests and powerful ones of the world did not want to love him. They did not belong to him and were not his members and brothers and sisters. Nevertheless, those who were capable of receiving his words loved him. Therefore those who love truth and righteousness would also love him and keep company with him, like Nicodemus, who loved Jesus in his heart on account of the truth, and came to him by night and was outwardly fearful of the world. So one will have many good friends who are unknown."

Love and Hate

The student said, "But it is difficult to be scorned by all the world." The teacher said, "What now seems difficult to you, you will afterward love the most."

The student said, "How can that be, or how can it happen, that I love what scorns me?" The teacher said, "Now you love earthly wisdom. But when you are clothed with heavenly wisdom, then you will see that the wisdom of all the world is mere folly, and that the world hates only your enemy, namely mortal life,[9] which you yourself also hate in your will. Then you will also begin to love scorn of the mortal body."

The student said, "But how can both of these occur at the same time, that one loves and hates oneself?" The teacher said, "What you love of yourself, you do not love as your own but as a love given from God. You love the divine ground in yourself, through which you love God's wisdom and miracles, together with your sisters and brothers. But what you hate of yourself is what you do in accordance with the you-ness, in which evil adheres to you. You do this because you would gladly shatter the I-ness, so that the shattered I-ness would become for you a completely divine ground. Love hates the I-ness because it is a deadly thing. They cannot stand together, because love possesses heaven and dwells in itself. But the I-ness possesses the world, together with its being, and also dwells in itself. Just as heaven governs the earth, and eternity governs time, so also love governs above the natural life."

The student said, "Dear teacher, tell me why must love and suffering, and friend and foe, coexist? Would it not be better to have only love?" The teacher said, "If love were not in suffering, it would have nothing that it could love. However, because love's being, which it loves, is in suffering and pain, just like the poor soul, love has cause to love its own being, and to rescue it from pain, so that it may be loved again. Further, it cannot be known what love is, if it did not have something that it could love."

The Qualities of Love

The student said, "What is love in its strength and its virtue, and its height and its greatness?" The teacher said, "Love's virtue is the nothing, and its power is through everything. Its height is as high as God, and its greatness is greater than God. Whoever finds love, finds nothing and everything."

The student said, "Oh dear teacher, tell me how may I understand that?" The teacher said, "When I said that love's virtue is the nothing, you will understand this when you go forth from all creatureliness, and become a nothing to all nature and creatureliness. Then you are in the Eternal One, which is God. Then you feel the highest virtue of love. When I said that love's strength is through everything, then you feel in your soul and body that when this great love is enkindled within you, it burns as no fire can. You will also see in all God's works how love has poured out itself into everything. It is the innermost and outermost ground in all things, inwardly according to the strength and outwardly according to the form. And when I further said that love's height is as high as God, this you should understand in yourself, that love leads you into itself as high as God is. You can see this in our dear Lord Jesus Christ, according to our humanness, whom love brought up to the highest throne in the strength of the Godhead. But when I also said that its greatness is greater than God, this is also true. For where God does not dwell, there love enters in. For when our dear Lord Jesus Christ stood in hell, hell was not God, but love was there and shattered death. Also, when you are in anguish, God is not that anguish. But God's love is there and leads you out of the anguish into God. When God hides in you, love is there and reveals God within you. And when I further said that whoever finds love finds nothing and everything, this is also true, because that person finds an unground, beyond nature and beyond the senses, that has no place as its abode and finds nothing that is like it. Therefore one can compare it with nothing, because it is deeper than a something. Therefore love is like a nothing to all things because it cannot be grasped. And because it is nothing, it is free from all things and is that single good, which one cannot describe. When I said that whoever finds love, finds everything, this is also true. Love has been the beginning of all things and governs all things. When you find it, you come into the ground out of which all things have arisen and in which they subsist. In love you are a king over all God's works."

The student said, "Dear teacher, tell me: where does love dwell in a person?" The teacher said, "Where the person does not dwell, there love has its residence."

The student said, "Where is it that one does not dwell in oneself?" The teacher said, "That is the thoroughly yielded soul. The soul dies to its own will, and it wills nothing more than what God wills. For insofar as the soul's own will is dead to itself, to that extent love has taken its place. Where previously self-will resided, there is now nothing. Where nothing is, only there God's love remains and operates."

The student said, "How may I grasp love without the death of my will?" The teacher said, "If it is the case that you want to grasp love, it will flee from you. But if you give yourself to it fully and completely, then you are dead to yourself with respect to your will. Then love becomes the life of your nature. Love does not kill you but rather makes you alive in accordance with its life. Then you live, but not to your will, but to its will, because your will becomes love's will. Then you are dead to yourself, yet you live to God."

The student said, "How is it that so few find love, yet all would gladly have it?" The teacher said, "They all seek it in something, as in an imagined idea in their own desire. Almost all of them have their own natural pleasure in their desire. Although love offers itself to them, it finds no place in them, for the imagination of their own will has set itself in love's place. So love wants to have in itself the imagination of their own pleasure, but love flees from them. For love lives only in the nothing, so they cannot find it."

The Fire of Love

The student said, "What is love's official duty in the nothing?" The teacher said, "This is love's official duty: that it incessantly penetrates into the something, and when it can find a place in the something that stands silent, love takes the something and rejoices in it with its fire-flaming love more than the sun in the world. Love's official charge is incessantly to kindle a fire in the something and burn up the something and hyperinflame itself with it."[10]

The student said, "Oh dear teacher, how shall I understand this?" The teacher said, "If it is the case that love were to kindle a fire in you, you would feel how it burns away your I-ness and how it greatly rejoices in your fire, so that you would rather permit yourself to be killed than to reenter your something. Furthermore, love's flame is so great that it will not leave you. Even if it costs you your temporal life, love goes into death with you in its fire. Even if you enter into hell, love would shatter hell for your sake."

The student said, "Dear teacher, I can no longer endure being in error. How can I find the nearest path to love?" The teacher said, "Go where the path is the hardest, and take for yourself what the world throws away. Do not do what the world does. In all things go contrary to the world, so that you might come to the nearest path to love."

The student said, "If it is the case that I were to go contrary to the world in all things, I would have to stand in sheer misery and disquiet, and I would be considered foolish." The teacher said, "I would not enjoin you to do injury to anyone. But the world loves only deceit and vanity and goes on the wrong path. If you wish to be in opposition to its path in all things, then go only on the right path. For the right path is contrary to all the world's paths. But you say that you will stand in sheer anguish. That happens according to the flesh; it gives you cause for persistent repentance. And in such anguish, love is supremely dear as it blows on the fire." You say, moreover, that you would be considered foolish. That is true, for the path to the love of God is a folly to the world, but wisdom to the children of God. When the world sees such love-fire in God's children, it says they are foolish. But to the children of God this love-fire is the greatest treasure. For no life can ever express, and no mouth can ever describe, the fire of the inflaming love of God. It is whiter than the sun and sweeter than any honey and stronger than any food or drink, and also lovelier than all joys of this world. Whoever attains this is wealthier than any king on earth and nobler than any emperor could be, and stronger than all might."

Heaven and Hell Are Everywhere

The student further questioned the teacher, "Where does the soul travel when the body dies, whether it be holy or damned?" The teacher said, "The soul cannot journey outward. Rather the external, mortal life, together with the body, only separate themselves from it. Previously the soul had heaven and hell within it; as it is written, the reign of God does not come with outward appearance. Nor can one say, 'Look here!' or 'There it is.' For look, the reign of God is within you (Luke 17:20–21). Whichever is revealed in the soul, whether heaven or hell, that is where it dwells."

The student said, "Does the soul not go into heaven or hell just as someone enters a house, or as someone enters another world through a hole?" The teacher said, "No, there is no entering in such a manner, for heaven and hell are present everywhere. There is only a turning of the will, either into God's love or wrath. This happens in the time of the body, of which St. Paul says, 'Our life is in heaven' (Phil. 3:20). And Christ also said, 'My sheep hear my voice, and I know them, and they follow me, and I give them eternal life, and no one will snatch them from my hand' (John 10:27–28)."

The student said, "How does this entering of the will into heaven or hell happen?" The teacher said, "When the will gives itself thoroughly to God, then the soul sinks outside itself, beyond all ground and place, to where God alone is revealed and works and wills. Then the soul becomes to itself a nothing, with respect to its will. Then God works and wills in it, and God dwells in its yielded will. By this the soul is made holy so that it comes into divine rest. When the body breaks up, the soul is permeated with divine love and fully illuminated with God's light, as fire glows through iron by which the iron loses its darkness. This is the hand of Christ. When God's love fully dwells throughout the soul and is a shining light and new life in it, then it is in heaven, and a temple of the Holy Spirit, and is itself God's heaven in which God dwells. But the godless soul does not wish to go within time into divine yieldedness of its will. Instead, it continually goes only into its own longing and desire, into vanity and falsehood, into the devil's will. It takes into itself only evil, lying, pride, greed, envy, and wrath, and yields its will to them. This same vanity is revealed and works in the soul and permeates it completely, as fire does iron. The soul cannot come to divine rest, for God's wrath is revealed in it. So when the body separates from the soul, eternal remorse and despair begin. For the soul perceives that it has become such a vain, anxious abomination, and it is ashamed. The soul perceives that it should force its way toward God with its false will. In fact, it is unable, because the soul is imprisoned in wrath, and is itself a vain wrath in which it has locked itself up by its false desires, which it has aroused in itself. Because God's light does not shine in the soul, and God's love does not touch it, it is a great darkness and a painful, anxious fire-torment. It bears hell within itself and cannot see the light of God. Therefore the soul dwells within itself in hell; no entering is permitted. Whatever it is in, it is in hell. If it could swing up many hundred thousand miles away from its place, it would still be in such torment and darkness."

But They Are Not Perceived

The student said, "How is it then that the holy soul cannot perfectly perceive such light and great joy within this time, and that the godless does not feel hell, since both are in a person, even though only one works in a person?" The teacher said, "The reign of heaven is operative and perceptible in the holy ones in their faith. They feel God's love in their faith, through which the will gives itself to God. But the natural life is enveloped in flesh and blood and stands in contrast to the wrath of God, enveloped by the vain pleasure of this world that constantly pervades the external mortal life. On one side is the world, on another side is the devil, and on the third side is the curse of God's wrath. These pervade and sift flesh and blood. Therefore the soul often stands in anguish when hell presses on it and wishes to reveal itself in the soul. But the soul sinks into the hope of divine grace, and stands as a beautiful rose among the thorns until the reign of this world falls away from it in the death of the body. Then, when nothing more hinders the soul, it will be all the more truly revealed in God's love. The soul must transform time in this world with Christ. Christ redeems the soul from its own hell, in that Christ pervades it with his love and stands by it in hell and transforms its hell into heaven. But you say, 'Why does the godless one not feel hell in this time?' I say, 'The godless one indeed feels hell in their false conscience but does not understand it, because they still have the earthly vanity and are in love with it, have joy and pleasure in it.' In addition, the external life still has the light of external nature in which the soul is entertained, and therefore that pain cannot be revealed. But when the body dies, the soul can no longer enjoy such temporal pleasure, and the light of external nature is extinguished. Then the soul stands in eternal thirst and hunger for the vanity that it had been enamored with here, but it can attain to nothing but a false, limited will. In this life the soul had too much vanity, and yet was not content; then it had too little, and therefore it is in eternal hunger and thirst for vanity, evil, and frivolity. It would gladly commit more evil, but has nothing in which or with which it can complete it. So the completion happens only in the soul itself. Such hellish hunger and thirst cannot be fully manifest in the soul until the body with which it prostituted itself dies. The body had coupled itself with the soul, and the soul lusted for the body."

The student spoke, "Since heaven and hell are in conflict within us in this time, and since God is thus close to us, where then do the angels and devils dwell in such time?" The teacher said, "Where you do not dwell according to your own self and will, there the angels dwell with you and everywhere. Where you dwell according to your own self and will, there the devils dwell with you and everywhere."

The student said, "I do not understand that." The teacher said, "Where God's will wills in a thing, there God is revealed. In such a revelation the angels also dwell. Where God does not will in a thing with the thing's will, God is not revealed to the thing but dwells only in God's self, without the thing's cooperation. Then the thing's own will is in itself without God's will, and there the devils dwell, along with everything that is outside of God."

The student said, "So then how far are heaven and hell from each other?" The teacher said, "As day and night, as something and nothing. They are in each other, and each is to the other as a nothing. And yet they cause each other joy and suffering. Heaven is throughout the whole world and outside the world everywhere, without any separation, place, or location, and works through divine revelation only in itself. And in that into which heaven comes, or in that in which it is revealed, there God is revealed. For heaven is nothing other than a revelation of the Eternal One, where everything works and wills in silent love. Likewise hell is also throughout the whole world; it dwells and works also only in itself and in that which reveals hell's foundation, as in self and false willing. The visible world has both heaven and hell in itself. In accordance with this temporal life, however, the human person is only from this visible world, and therefore in this time of the external life, the person does not see the spiritual world. For the external world with its being is a covering in front of the spiritual world, just as the soul is covered with the body. But when the external person dies, then the spiritual world, in accordance with the soul, is revealed, either according to the eternal light with the holy angels or according to the eternal darkness with the devils."

Soul and Body

The student said, "Then what is an angel, or a person's soul, that it may be thus revealed in God's love or wrath?" The teacher said, "They are of the same origin, a piece from divine knowledge of divine will, originating from divine word and led into a pattern of divine love. They are from the ground of eternity from which light and darkness arise. As darkness is in the possessiveness of one's own desires, so light is in willing what God wills. Where the I-ness of the soul wills with God, there God's love is operative. In the self-presumption of the soul's will, God's will operates painfully and is a darkness, so that the light can become known. They are nothing other than a revelation of the divine will, either in light or darkness, of the characteristics of the spiritual world."

The student said, "Then what is a person's body?" The teacher said, "It is the visible world, an image and a being of all that is in the world. The visible world is a revelation of the inner spiritual world, manifested from the eternal light and from the eternal darkness, out of the spiritual fabric.[12] It is a pattern of eternity with which eternity has made itself visible, since self-will and yielded will interweave with one another, just as evil and good. The external person is also such a being, for God created the external person from the external world, and blew into the external person the interior spiritual world for a soul and rational life. Therefore the soul in the external world's being can receive and work evil and good."

When This World Ends

The student said, "What then will there be after this world, when all has passed away?" The teacher said, "Only material being ceases—the four elements, the sun, the moon, and the stars. Then the inner spiritual world will become fully visible and revealed. But whatever has been accomplished in this time through the spirit, whether evil or good, each work will separate itself either into the eternal light or into the eternal darkness, in accordance with its spiritual type. For what is born of each will, penetrates again into its likeness. Then the darkness will be called hell, as an eternal forgetting of all good. And the light will be called the reign of God, as an eternal joy and an eternal praise of the saints because they have been redeemed from such pain. The Last Judgment is a kindling of the fire in accordance with God's love and wrath. In it the material of all being passes away, and each fire will draw into itself its own, as a being of its likeness. What is born in God's love draws the love-fire of God into itself, in which it will also burn in accordance with the manner of love, and will give itself into the same being. But what is accomplished in God's wrath according to darkness draws painfulness into itself and consumes the false being. Only the painful shall remain in its own image and form."

The Resurrected Body

The student asked, "In what material or form will our bodies be resurrected?" The teacher said, "It was sown as a natural, coarse, and elemental body, which is like the external elements in this time. In this same coarse body there is a subtle strength, just as there is a subtle, good strength in the earth, which is comparable to the sun and unites with it; at the beginning of time the sun also originated from divine strength, from which the good strength of the body is also taken. This good strength of the mortal body will come again and remain forever, or live in a beautiful, transparent, crystalline, material characteristic in spiritual flesh and blood. Then, just as the good strength of the earth, so also will the earth itself be crystalline. Then the divine light will shine in all beings. And as the coarse earth will pass away and not return, so likewise the coarse flesh of human-kind will pass away and not live eternally. But all of the body must come into judgment. In judgment everything must be separated through the fire, both the earth and the ashes of the human body. Then when God will move the spiritual world once again, each spirit will again draw its spiritual being to itself. A good spirit and soul draws to itself its good being, and an evil spirit and soul draws its evil being. But one must understand that this is only a substantial, material power, for being is sheer power, like a material transform-ing substance, for the coarseness in all things will pass away."

The student said, "So we shall not rise with the visible bodies and live in them eternally?" The teacher said, "When the visible world passes away, all that has been external and originated from it will pass away. Only the heavenly, crystalline manner and form of the world remains. Likewise only the spiritual earth remains from the person. For the person will be completely like the spiritual world that is now still hidden."

All of One Gender

The student said, "In the spiritual life, will there also be husband and wife, or children, or relatives? Will they associate with one another as happened here?" The teacher said, "How fleshly minded you are! There will be neither husband nor wife, but all will be only like the angels of God: male virgins, who are not daughter, son, brother, nor sister, but rather all of one gender. In Christ they are all simply one, like a tree in its branches, and yet separate creatures; but God all in all. Then there will be a spiritual knowledge of what each has been and what each has done. But there will be no more possessiveness or desire to be a possessive being."

Variety of Reward

The student asked, "Will all of them alike enjoy eternal joy and glorification?" The teacher said, "Scripture says, 'Such as a people is, such is their God.' Again: 'With the holy you are holy, and with the perverse you are perverse.' (Pss. 18:26–27). And St. Paul writes, 'In the resurrection they will surpass one another, as the sun, moon, and stars' (1 Cor. 15:41). So know that they will all enjoy divine working, but their strength and illumination will be very dissimilar. Each one will be clothed with power in accordance with one's anguished working in this time. For the anguished working of the creature of this time is an opening and a birthing of divine power, through which God's power is set in motion and becomes operative. Those who have worked with Christ in this time and not in fleshly pleasure will have a great power and beautiful glorification, both within and upon them. But others who only awaited a calculated satisfaction, and who served the god of the belly and converted only at the end and came to grace, will not have so great a power and illumination. Therefore there will be a differentiation among them, as among sun, moon, and stars, and as among the flowers of the field in their beauty, power, and virtue."

The Final Judgment

The student said, "How or by whom will the world be judged?" The teacher said, "By divine movement through the person and Spirit of Christ who, through the word of God that became human, will separate what does not belong to Christ and will fully reveal Christ's reign in the place where this world stands. For the movement of the separation occurs everywhere the same."

The student said, "Then where will the devils and the damned be cast forth, since the place of this entire world is the realm of Christ and will be glorified? Will they be driven outside of the place of this world, or will Christ have and reveal his sovereignty outside of the place of this world?" The teacher said, "Hell will remain in the place of this world everywhere, but hidden to the realm of heaven, as the night is hidden in the day. The light will shine eternally in the darkness, and the darkness cannot grasp it (John 1:5). Thus the light is the realm of Christ, and the darkness is hell, in which the devils and the godless dwell. They will therefore be suppressed in the reign of Christ and set up in disgrace as a footstool."

The student said, "How will all the people be brought before judgment?" The teacher said, "The eternal word of God, out of which all spiritual, creaturely life has come, will set itself in motion at that hour, in accordance with love and wrath in all life. This word is from eternity and will draw the creature before the judgment of Christ. Through such a movement of the word, life will be revealed in all its works, and each one will see and feel their sentence and judgment within. For the judgment will be revealed in the soul immediately upon the death of the human body. The Last Judgment is merely a return of the spiritual body and a separation of the world. For in the being of the world and in the body, the evil must be separated from the good, each thing to its eternal entrance and vessel. And this is a revelation of the hiddenness of God in all being and life."

The student said, "How will the sentence be passed?" The teacher said, "Look at the words of Christ, who will say to those on his right, 'Come, you blessed of my Father, inherit the reign that from the beginning of the world was prepared for you. For I was hungry and you fed me. I was thirsty and you gave me drink. I was a stranger and you offered me shelter. I was naked and you clothed me. I was sick and imprisoned, and you visited me and came to me.' And they will answer, 'When did we see you hungry, thirsty, a stranger, naked, sick, and imprisoned, and therefore served you?'

And the King will answer and say to them, 'What you did to these, the least of my family [brothers], you did to me.' And to the godless on the left he will say, 'Go away from me, you who are cursed, into the eternal fire that was prepared for the devil and his angels. I was hungry, thirsty, a stranger, naked, sick, and imprisoned, and you did not serve me.' And they will answer him and say, 'So when did we see you and not serve you?' Then he will answer, 'Truly I say to you, what you did not do to one of these the least, you did not do to me.' And they will go into the eternal pain, but the righteous will go into the eternal life" (Matt. 25:34–46).

Christ in the Christian

The student said, "Dear teacher, tell me why Christ says, 'What you have done to the least of these you have done to me, and what you have not done to them you have not done to me'? How does one do such to Christ so that it happens to Christ himself?" The teacher said, "Christ lives substantially in the faith of those who have given themselves fully to him. Christ gives them his flesh as food and his blood as drink, and thus possesses the ground of their faith in accordance with the inwardness of the person. Therefore a Christian is called a branch on Christ's vine and is called a Christian, because Christ dwells spiritually in that person. And what one does to such a Christian in his bodily needs one does to Christ, who dwells in that person. For such a Christian is not her or his own, but is fully given to Christ, and is Christ's property; therefore this happens to Christ himself. And whoever withdraws one's hand from such needy Christians and will not serve such a one in need pushes Christ away, and despises him in his members. When a poor person who belongs to Christ asks of you, and you deny it to that person in his or her need, you have denied it to Christ himself. Whoever does injury to such a Christian person does injury to Christ. When one disgraces, derides, reviles, and pushes away such a person, one does all this to Christ. But whoever receives, feeds, clothes, aids, gives drink, and hastens to help one in need, one does this to Christ and to members of Christ's own body. So one does it to Christ himself, if one is a Christian. For in Christ we are simply one, like a tree with its branches."

The Fate of Oppressors

The student said, "On the day of such judgment, how will these endure, who torment the poor and wretched and suck the sweat out of them, oppress them, and drag them off by force, and regard them as trash underfoot, only to consume ruthlessly the sweat of the poor in fleshly desires with arrogance and haughtiness?" The teacher said, "All these do it to Christ himself and deserve Christ's strict judgment. For thus they lay their hands on Christ, persecute him in his members, and moreover help the devil to increase his reign, and through such oppression they draw the poor away from Christ, so that the devil seeks an easy way to fill his belly. Yes, they who ceaselessly oppose the reign of Christ in love do nothing other than what the devil himself does. For all who do not turn to Christ with all their heart and serve Christ must enter into the hellish fire in which such vain self-centeredness is."

Religious Persecution and War

The student said, "How will those endure who in this time dispute over the reign of Christ, and because of this persecute, defame, shame, and revile one another?" The teacher said, "All these have never yet known Christ, and stand only in the figure of how heaven and hell struggle with one another for victory.[13] All the heightening of arrogance in which one disputes about mere opinions is a likeness of possessiveness. Whoever does not have faith and humility and does not stand in the Spirit of Christ is armed only with the wrath of God, and serves life for the victory by apparent self-centeredness, namely the realm of darkness and the wrath of God. For all self-centeredness will be given to the darkness, as will their useless wrangling, through which they seek not love but only illusory self-centeredness that shows itself in their opinions. Through them they cause princes to wage war for the sake of such airy opinions. With their mere ideas they storm and lay waste to land and people. All these belong in judgment for the separation of false and true. Then all images and opinions will cease. All God's children will walk in the love of Christ, who will walk in us. All that in this time of strife is not zealous for the Spirit of Christ and does not desire to promote only love, but rather seeks in strife its own profit, is of the devil and belongs in the darkness and will be separated from Christ. For in heaven everything serves God, its creator, with humility."

Strife Reveals Truth but Yields to Joy

The student said, "Then why does God permit such strife in this time?" The teacher said, "Life stands in strife, so that it may be revealed, experienced, and discovered, and so that wisdom may be distinguished and known. It serves for the eternal joy of victory. For among the saints in Christ, there will arise a great praise that Christ has overcome the darkness and all self-centeredness of nature within them, and that they are redeemed from the strife. They will rejoice eternally when they will realize how the godless will be recompensed. Therefore God permits all things to stand in free will, so that the eternal sovereignty in accordance with love and wrath, and light and darkness, may be revealed and known. Thus each life may cause and awaken its own judgment within itself. For what is now a strife and a pain to the saints in their misery will be transformed into a great joy for them. What is a delight and a joy to the godless in this world will be changed into eternal pain and shame. Therefore for the saints, their joy must arise from death, just as the light of a candle must arise through the death and consumption in the fire, so that the life therefore becomes free from the painfulness of nature and possesses another world. Just as light has a completely different characteristic from fire and gives of itself, but the fire takes of itself and consumes itself, so also the holy life of gentleness sprouts forth through the death in which the self-will dies. Then only God's love governs and acts all in all. For thus the Eternal assumed sensitivity and became amicable, and with sensitivity led itself forth again through death into the great realm of joy, so that there might be an eternal play in the unending unity, and an eternal cause for the realm of joy. Pain therefore must be a ground and cause of such motion."

And in this lies the mystery of the hidden wisdom of God. "Whoever asks receives, whoever seeks finds, and to one who knocks it will be opened" (Matt. 7.7). The grace of our Lord Jesus Christ and the love of God and the communion of the Holy Spirit be with us all. Amen.[14]

THE NEW BIRTH

T HE NEW BIRTH dates from 1622 and, like *Life Beyond the Senses*, was printed as part of *The Way to Christ*.[1] The text's title in German is rather redundant: literally, *The New Rebirth* (*Das neue Wiedergeburt*). Jakob Boehme takes as his starting point the familiar words of Jesus in the Gospel according to John 3:5, which says that one must be born anew to enter the reign of God, but Boehme then moves in a direction that differs in significant ways from most modern born–again Christians.

In *The New Birth* the reader will recognize some common themes from *Life Beyond the Senses*. Boehme's cosmology is consistent throughout both writings. Boehme perceives the world as having an underlying intensity that can be a force for destruction or bliss. Fire and light, or wrath and love, are not the same, and yet they are one in nature. When this nature is manifested in light, it yields joy and bliss. Boehme's universe consists of three worlds. The first two worlds are spiritual antagonists: the light-world and the fire- (or dark-) world. The third world is visible, tangible materiality. The two spiritual worlds impinge upon the third, visible world. According to the astrology and alchemy that were dominant in Boehme's world, the visible world was made up of the four elements—earth, air, fire, and water—and was influenced by the stars. Boehme suggests each element has within it a "star" that determines its quality. Just as this inward star shapes the element, the mind of the soul influences the soul as it is manifested in the concrete bodily life.

As in *Life Beyond the Senses*, Boehme uses the metaphor of raising the soul's mind by swinging it upward in an arc. He returns to the centrality of the will, a theme that he develops further. Once again he describes the primordial unity of all being, and notes that opposites mutually dwell in one another—heaven and hell, light and dark, eternity and time. The outward person is conditioned by time and external circumstances, but inwardly a person lives in eternity, unhindered by these limitations. There is a mutual permeation of the outer and the inner: within the inward realm of eternity, light and darkness mutually permeate, and yet neither possesses the other. Again he declares that heaven is a place of playfulness and joy, in contrast to the violence that dominates this world, which is the third world.

Toward the end of *The New Birth*, Boehme states a kind of summary of this essay and, it could be argued, his whole corpus. He writes that the whole Christian religion consists in coming to know our original state of unity, how we have departed from it, our current disunity and strife, and how we are renewed.

These are the great themes toward which he is perpetually attracted. Thus *The New Birth* can be seen as the fulcrum of Jakob Boehme's thought, since in this essay he concerns himself with "how to come out of disunity and vanity and to enter again into one tree out of which we all have come in Adam, which tree is Christ in us."

As he reflects on this process of returning to primordial unity, the essay takes on particular emphasis regarding the initial unity, the fall away from that oneness, and the restoration of that unity through the new birth. In Adam's original state, for example, he ate the fruit of paradise, which was simultaneously spiritual and corporeal. Because it was not assimilated like food as we know it, this fruit did not require teeth to eat it or digestive organs to derive its benefits. Both our teeth and our organs of digestion and elimination are a result of Adam's fall. Boehme's low esteem for what he regards as a coarse, bestial form of digestion is shown in his colorful description of the intestines as a maggot sack—perhaps drawn from personal observation of carcasses, given the frequency of intestinal worms in most mammals in his day. Also in paradise, Adam did not yet know the distinction between good and evil, because he had not eaten from the forbidden tree of the knowledge of good and evil. Knowledge of those distinctions, however, revealed other differences as well; for instance, before his fall, Adam felt neither heat nor cold. All was in balance, until Adam's desire for his own will upset the equilibrium.

In the fall into sin, the soul becomes inwardly like a devil, because the devil's realm is the dark, fiery world that can permeate the inner life. The soul takes an outward body, like the animals, which have organs for digestion and reproduction. Boehme indicates that both inwardly and outwardly, Adam and Eve have lost the angelic state. Yet redemption is possible in both the inward and outward dimensions. Ultimately, not even the devil is lost for Boehme; God's redemptive act in the incarnation had more than just a human goal. In Boehme's view, not only is death overcome, but hell itself is transformed, and even the devil is reconciled to God through divine love.

In Christian theology, there are close relationships between a thinker's understanding of the human condition and its problems, the possibilities for salvation, and the nature of Christ as redeemer. In this treatise Boehme draws a distinction between mortal flesh and heavenly corporeality; the latter includes flesh and blood, but not of the coarse sort that followed upon Adam's disobedience. This notion helps us to understand Boehme's theological understanding of Christ and how it was that Christ achieved redemption for humankind. In Christ's heavenly corporeality, the blood that he shed in his death on the cross communicates its properties to external human blood, transforming the inner hell, where people live in the wrath of God, into an inner heaven, where there is joy and playfulness. Thus,

Boehme claims, the new birth happens in flesh and blood but not in mortal flesh. When he claims that the mortal person falls and sins, but not the righteous, Boehme is maintaining that distinction between these two kinds of flesh and blood. The human body stands at the border between earthly and heavenly forms of being.

For Boehme, however, the new birth remains fundamentally a matter of the will. The new birth means a new will, a death of the old will and its desires. It is the will that takes in Christ's heavenly corporeality. Christ's shed blood restores the balance, equilibrium, and harmony that prevailed in paradise. Then this awakened, heavenly, spiritual body is Christ's member and a temple of the Holy Spirit. This person eats Christ's holy being, which enkindles a great love.

This language of eating is further reflected in Boehme's explanation of the sacrament of the Lord's Supper. What the saints, as Boehme calls them, apprehend in the bread and wine of communion is an inner spiritual reality that is experienced as something concrete, even though it is not material. They eat of Christ's holy being. The inner person is the container that receives the holy being that Christ gives. Thus it is the person who is transmuted, rather than the bread and cup of communion being filled with the presence of Christ. What makes the transmutation possible is divine love moving a person's will to choose to live in the world of light and love, rather than in the world of wrath.[2]

But there are limits to the fullness of our restoration in this life. The holy, precious pearl, by which Boehme means complete reunion with Sophia, the Wisdom of God, is not fully given in this life because the outward part of the soul is not reborn but persists in its bond to vanity. Sophia hides in Christ's heavenly humanity and cannot draw near to such vanity. Because the outward part of the soul remains unregenerate, Boehme states that a struggle continues between the fleshly person and the inward, spiritual person, echoing the language of the apostle Paul in Galatians 5:17.

This inner struggle is mirrored in the outer world. Boehme repeats his distinction between genuine Christians and mere "mouth-

Christians," who may say the traditional words but do not perform the proper actions of a real Christian. Christianity is a matter of doing, not simply speaking. The stone churches, as he calls them, are filled with hypocrisy, mere history and husk, as opposed to inner experience.

The stone churches quarrel and even make war about mere religious opinions. A true Christian can live among such sects, but belongs to none of them. Those who experience the new birth do not fight about religion. They have "a single knowledge, which is Christ within." Such knowledge is nonpossessive. It does not lead to violence because it is yielded to God's will alone. Faith enveloped in this hope is beyond sectarian quarreling. Those who live in the new birth do not concern themselves with such disputes but instead live in love. Heaven, which they already experience inwardly, is about play and joy, not violence:

> We must not dispute about anything nor have any conflict. Let each exert himself or herself to be able to enter once again into the love of God and of one's brothers and sisters.

THE NEW BIRTH

CHAPTER I

The New Birth Is Within

Christ speaks, "Unless you are converted and become as children, you will not see the reign of God" (Matt. 18:3). And again he says to Nicodemus, "Unless someone is born anew from water and Spirit, one cannot enter the reign of God, for what is born of flesh is flesh, and what is born of Spirit is Spirit" (John 3:5–6). The scripture clearly witnesses that the fleshly, natural person takes nothing from the Spirit of God. For such a person it is folly, and such a person cannot comprehend.

However, even though we all have flesh and blood, and therefore are mortal, as is evident, at the same time scripture says that we are also a temple of the Holy Spirit, who dwells in us (1 Cor. 6:19). And scripture says that the reign of God is inwardly in us (Luke 17:21), indeed that Christ must gain a form in us (Gal. 4:19), and also that Christ wishes to give his flesh for food and his blood for drink. And scripture says further that whoever does not eat the flesh of the Son of Man has no life in Christ (John 6:53). So therefore we must earnestly reflect what kind of person is in us, that is similar to and capable of the Godhead.

For it cannot be said, concerning the mortal flesh, which returns to earth and lives in the vanity of this world, and always lusts contrary to God, that it is the temple of the Holy Spirit, much less can it be said that the new rebirth happens in this earthly flesh, because it dies and decomposes, besides it is a constant habitation of sin.

Yet it remains true, that a true Christian is born forth of Christ, and that this new birth is a temple of the Holy Spirit, who dwells in us. And only the new person who is born from Christ enjoys the flesh and blood of Christ. So it is not a simple thing to be a Christian. Christianity does not stand in the history that we only know, and that we appropriate as knowledge, so that we merely say, "Christ has died for us and has broken death within us and has made death into life. He has paid for us the debt; we may take comfort in this and firmly believe that it has happened."

Sin

For we find in ourselves that sin in the flesh is lively, desirous, and active, and that it is efficacious. Therefore the new birth from Christ must be something else, so that it does not cooperate with the sinful flesh, and does not want sins.

For St. Paul says, "To those who are in Christ there is nothing damnable" (Rom. 8:1). And further, should we, we who are Christians, nevertheless be found to be sinners? Far from it! (Gal. 2:17). Therefore we have died to sin.[3] Also the person of sin is not a temple of the Holy Spirit. And there is no person who does not sin. For scripture says, "God has locked up everyone under sin" (Rom. 11:32). Again: "If you would keep account of sin, no living person is righteous in your presence."[4] "The righteous falls seven times a day" (Prov. 24:16), but this may not be understood that the righteous one falls and sins, rather the mortal one.[5]

For the righteousness of a Christian is in Christ, who cannot sin. For St. Paul says, "Our life is in heaven from which we await the Savior Jesus Christ" (Phil. 3:20). If our life is in heaven, then heaven must be in us. Christ dwells in heaven. If we are his temple, so the same heaven must be in us.

Since, moreover, sin assails us within, by means of which the devil has access to us and within us, therefore hell must also be within us, for the devil dwells in hell. And wherever he is, he is in hell and cannot come out. And if he possesses a person, then the devil dwells in the person, in hell, as in God's wrath.

The Will Must Be Reborn

Now we must consider more fully what and how a person is. We must consider whether a true Christian is not only a new historical person, whether it suffices that we confess and believe in Christ, that Christ is the Son of God and has paid the price for us. For an outwardly imputed righteousness is not valid, in which we merely believe that it happened. Rather, an inborn, a childlike righteousness is valid. Just as the flesh must die, so the life and the will of sin must die. It must become as a child who knows nothing and yearns only for the mother who gave it birth. Therefore the will of a Christian must completely enter again into the mother, that is, the Spirit of Christ, and become a child in its selfhood, its self-willing, and its ability. There, only in the mother, the will and desire are set in order, and from the Spirit of Christ a new will and obedience in righteousness must arise from death, a will that no longer wants sin.

The will, insofar as it permits vanity into itself and desires it,[6] is not reborn. And moreover, in those who are reborn a will similarly remains that yearns for vanity and sins. Therefore it is appropriate for us to consider how we picture the human person and to consider how the new birth occurs. For the new birth does not happen in mortal flesh, and yet it truly happens within us in flesh and blood, in water and spirit, as the scripture says.

Therefore we must properly consider what kind of person is within us, who is a member of Christ and a temple of God, who dwells in heaven. And then also we must consider what kind of person it is who dwells only in the outer world, what kind of person it is whom the devil governs and drives. For the devil cannot govern and drive the temple of Christ, therefore there is no opportunity for the devil in mortal flesh. And yet there are not three persons inside one another, but only one unified person.

Human Origins: Light and Darkness, Time and Eternity

If we want to consider such things, then we must ponder time and eternity, and how they are in one another, namely light and darkness, good and evil, especially the human origin and lineage.

This is also to be considered. We look at the outer world, with stars and the four elements, in which the person and all creatures live. This is not God and is not called God, yet God dwells within it, but the being of the outer world does not grasp God. Therefore we also see how the light shines in the darkness, and the darkness does not grasp the light, and yet one dwells within the other.[7] And so we also have an example of this in the four elements, which were in their origin only one element, which is neither hot nor cold, neither dry nor wet, and yet separates itself with the movement into four properties, namely, fire, air, water, and earth.

Who would want to believe that fire could give birth to water, and that the origin of fire could be in water, if we did not see it with our own eyes in lightning, and if we did not discover in the living things that the essential fire in the body dwells in the blood, and that the blood is the mother of the essential fire, and that the fire is the father of the blood?

For just as God dwells in the world, and fills everything, and yet possesses nothing—and just as fire dwells in water and yet does not possess it, and just as light dwells in darkness and yet does not possess the darkness, and day in night and night in day, and time in eternity and eternity in time—thus humankind was similarly created. According to the outward humanity, the person is time and is in time, and time is the outer world, which is also the outer person. And the inner person is eternity and the spiritual time and world, which also stands in light and darkness, that is, in God's love according to the eternal light, and in God's wrath according to the eternal darkness. That which is revealed in a person, therein dwells the person's spirit, either in darkness or in light. Both are within, the light and the darkness. Each one dwells in itself; neither possesses the other.

If either light or darkness invades the other and wants to possess the other, then the other loses its rights and power.[8] The one that suffers invasion loses its power. For if the light is revealed in the darkness, the darkness loses its dark quality, and is not recognized as darkness. And furthermore, if the darkness rises into the light and obtains power, so the light along with its power is extinguished.

Such a thing in the human condition should be contemplated by us. The eternal darkness in the soul is hell, like a torment of anxiety, which is called the wrath of God. And the eternal light in the soul is the reign of heaven, because the fiery, dark anxiety is transformed into a joy.

For just as the nature of the anxiety in the darkness is a cause of sorrow, so the nature of anxiety in the light is a cause of considerable and moving joy. For the quality in the light and the quality in the dark is only one unified quality, only one nature, as the fire and the light are only one nature, and yet they yield a powerful difference. One dwells in the other and gives birth to the other, and yet is not the other. Fire is painful and destructive, and the light is friendly, giving, strong, full of joy, a delightful bliss.

Three Worlds

Thus we should consider the human condition: a person stands and lives in three worlds. The one is the eternal dark-world, the center of eternal nature, which gives birth to the fire, namely the torment of anxiety. And the second is the eternal light-world, which gives birth to the eternal joy, and is the divine dwelling-place, in which the Spirit of God dwells, in which the Spirit of Christ takes on human essence and drives out the darkness, so that it must be a cause of joy in the Spirit of Christ in the light. The third world is the outward, visible world, in the four elements and the visible stars. Just as each element has within itself a star according to the element's characteristic, from which the desire and characteristic arise, so it is with the mind of the soul.

Therefore understand this: the fire in the light is a love-fire, a desire of gentleness and the realm of joy. And the fire in the darkness is a fire of anxiety; it is painful and inimical, and distasteful in its essence. The fire of the light is a good taste, and the taste of the darkness in its essence is thoroughly distasteful and inimical. For the forms of this fire all stand in the greatest anxiety.

CHAPTER 2

Creation, External and Internal

Now we must consider how humankind was created. Moses rightly said, "God created the person according to God's image, indeed in the image of God, God created the person" (Gen. 1:27). We understand this from the standpoint of the eternal and temporal birth: from the standpoint of the inner spiritual world, which God blew into the person in the created, external image, and then from the standpoint of the being of the inner spiritual world, which is holy.

For just as in the outer world there is a nature and being, therefore also in the inner spiritual world there is a nature and being, which is spiritual, out of which the external world is exhaled and birthed out of light and darkness, and then created in a beginning and time. And out of the being of the inner and outer world, the person was created in a likeness, in accordance with the birth, and out of the birth of all being. The body is a border of the earth and also a border of heavenly being.[9] For the earth is exhaled or spoken out of the dark- and light-world. Out of this dark- and light-world the human being was fashioned and created in the creative utterance, that is, in eternal desire, into an image, out of time and eternity.

This image was in the inner and spiritual element, out of which the four elements go forth and are born. Paradise was of the unified element, for the characteristics of the nature, out of the fire-dark world and the light-world, were all in equal balance, measure, and weight. None of them was particularly more manifest than the other. Therefore there was no fragility therein. No characteristic outdid the other; there was no strife or antipathy among the powers and the characteristics.

Into this created image God breathed the spirit and breath of understanding out of all three worlds, as into one unified soul, which in respect to the inner dark- and fire-world belongs to that eternal spiritual nature in accordance with which God is named a strong, jealous God and a consuming fire.

This, then, is the eternal, creaturely, great soul, a magical fire-breath in which the fire is the cause of life, out of the great power of transformation.[10] In this characteristic is the wrath of God, as well as the eternal darkness, insofar as the fire gives no light.

The second characteristic of the breath of God is the source-spirit of light, out of the great, fiery love-desire, and out of the great gentleness,[11] according to which God is named a loving, merciful God. In this source-spirit the true Spirit of understanding and life stands in strength.

For just as a light shines out of each fire, and the strength of understanding is recognized in the light, so the light-breath is attached to the fire-breath of God and was blown into the human image.

The third characteristic of the breath of God was the outward air, with the air-star. And in this characteristic of the breath of God were the life and stars of the outward being and body, which God blew into the person's nose. And just as time and eternity are attached to one another, and time is born out of eternity, so the inward breath of God is attached to the outward, and this threefold soul was blown simultaneously at once into the person. Each being of the body received the Spirit in accordance with its characteristic. Therefore outward flesh received the outward air with its stars for the purpose of a reasoning and growing life, for the revelation of the miracles of God. And the body of the light, or the heavenly being, received the breath of light, namely divine strength. This breath is called the Holy Spirit.

All Was in Balance in Paradise

The light pressed through the darkness, that is, the dark fire-breath, and also pressed through the outward air-breath and its star, and took the power of all the characteristics. Consequently the anxiety of the fire-breath in the inner characteristic that pertains to the soul neither could nor might be revealed. Neither could heat and cold, nor all of the other characteristics of the outward star, be revealed. The characteristics of all three worlds in soul and body stood in equal balance and weight. That which was inner and holy ruled through the outward, namely through the outward strengths of the outward life of the outward stars and the four elements.

This therefore was holy paradise. The human stood in heaven and also in the outer world, and was sovereign over all creatures of this world. Nothing could shatter the person.

And thus also was the earth, up until the curse of God. The holy characteristic of the spiritual world also sprouted throughout the earth, and bore holy, paradisiacal fruit, which the person could eat in such a magical and paradisiacal manner, that required no teeth or intestines in the body. Just as light swallows darkness, and fire swallows water, and yet is not filled with it, the first person had such a center in his mouth in the manner of eternity. And in such a magical way the person could also give birth to his own likeness without tearing or opening the body and spirit. It is like this: God gave birth to the outer world and did not tear God's self, but through desire, namely through the creative utterance, God fashioned the characteristic and endowed it with qualities, revealing it from the creative utterance, and led it into an image that was in accordance with the birth of the eternal spiritual world. Therefore, in like manner, the person was created as such an image and likeness, in accordance with time and eternity, but in an eternal, immortal life, which was without enmity and antipathy.

Imbalance Revealed Difference

But because the devil had been a prince and ruler in the location of this world, and because of his pride, he was shoved into the dark, anxious, painful, inimical characteristic and torture, into the fierceness of God. So the devil could not allow the human the honor of taking the devil's former place, which had been created in the spiritual world. So the devil directed his imagination into the created image of the human and made that which lusts, so that the characteristics of the dark-world, as well as the outer world, rose up in the human. As a result, these characteristics departed from such balance and equilibrium, so that one outweighed the other. Then the characteristics became evident, each in itself, and each lusted for its likeness, both the characteristics from the birth of the dark-world, and those from the birth of the light-world. Each wanted to eat from the mud of the earth, according to its hunger.[12]

Therefore evil and good were revealed in Adam. And in Adam, the hunger of the characteristics entered into the earth, out of which the characteristics of the body had been drawn. Therefore the creative power drew from the earth a kind of growth from which the characteristics could eat in their awakened vanities.[13]

Then this was possible: because the Spirit of the strong and great magical power of time and eternity was in Adam, out of which Spirit the earth with its characteristics was exhaled, therefore the creative power, namely the strong desire of the eternal nature, attracted the essence of earth.

Therefore God permitted the tree of the knowledge of good and evil to grow for Adam, in accordance with Adam's awakened characteristics. For the great power of the soul and body had caused this. So the human had to be tested, whether he would withstand by his own strengths in the face of the tempter, namely the devil, and in the face of eternal nature, or whether the soul would remain in the same balance in characteristics, in true yield-edness, under God's Spirit, as a ready tool of God's harmony, a play of the divine realm of joy. Upon this tool [or instrument] and in this soul, God's Spirit wished to play.[14] All of this was tried by means of this tree. And therefore God's strict commandment came and said, "Do not eat of this tree; on the day you eat from it you will surely die" (Gen. 2:17).

The Creation of Eve

But since God knew that the human would not withstand, and that the person would imagine and lust after evil and good, God spoke, "It is not good that the human should be alone. We will make a female helper for him, who will be with him." For God saw clearly that

Adam could not give birth magically because his delight had gone into vanity.

So now Moses says, "God allowed a deep sleep to fall on him and he fell asleep" (Gen. 2:21). That is, he no longer wished to remain in obedience to divine harmony, among the characteristics, so that he could have held silently to the Spirit of God as an instrument. Therefore God allowed him to fall from the divine harmony into his own harmony, that is, into the awakened characteristics, namely good and evil. There the spirit of Adam's soul entered.

Therefore Adam died to the angelic world in this sleep and reverted to the outward creative power.[15] And now here is what happened concerning the eternal image, as it pertains to God's birthing power. Here Adam's angelic form and power lay on the ground, and he fell into powerlessness. So out of Adam, God made the woman by means of the creative power, from the Venus matrix, that is, from the characteristic wherein Adam had in himself the female birth-giver: two from one body. And God separated the characteristics of the transforming substances, namely in the element of the watery constellation and of the fiery constellation, not completely in being but rather in spirit, namely the watery soul and the fiery soul, and yet it is only one; but the characteristic of the transforming substances was separated. The love and desire for self was taken from Adam and formed into a woman, according to his likeness. And therefore now the man desires the woman's matrix so powerfully. And the woman desires the man's *limbus*, namely the fire-element, the primordial condition of the true soul, in which the transforming substance of the fire is understood. Then the two were one in Adam, and therein stood the magical birth.

When Eve was made from Adam in his sleep, Adam and Eve were now set in order for the outward, natural life. Then the members for bestial reproduction were given to them, as well as the earthly digestive system in which they could pack vanity and live like the beasts.[16] On account of this, the poor soul, imprisoned in vanity, is still today ashamed of itself, because it received such a bestial, monstrous form for its body, as is evident. Human shame has originated from this, so that the human is ashamed of his or her body and also of the naked form, so that a person must borrow clothing from the earthly creatures, because humankind has lost its angelic clothing and has changed into a beast. This clothing indicates sufficiently that a person is not at home with this awakened vanity,[17] in that the person now notices heat and cold. For vanity along with the false clothing must leave the soul again and pass away.

Eating the Forbidden Fruit

And as Adam awoke from the sleep, he saw his wife and recognized her, because she came from him. For he had not yet eaten with the mouth of vanity, but only with the imagination, desire, and pleasure. And the first desire of Eve was that she wanted to eat from the tree of vanity, of evil and good, of which the devil in the form of a serpent fully persuaded her: "Your eyes will be opened, and you will be like God" (Gen. 3:5).

All of this was lies and truth. But he did not say to her that she would thereby lose the divine light and strength. He said only that her eyes would become open, that she would be able to taste, sample, and know good and evil, as he had done. He also did not say that heat and cold would grow in her and that the characteristic of the outer stars would rule powerfully in the flesh and in the soul's mind.

The devil's only intent was that the angelic image, namely the being of the inner, spiritual world, might fade away in them, so that they must live subject to coarse earthliness and the stars. He knew very well that when the outer world would perish, then the soul would be with him in the darkness. For he saw that the body would die, which he also knew from what God had said. Therefore he presumed that he would yet be a sovereign in eternity in the place of this world, in his false form that he had taken on. In this way he deceived humankind.

When Adam and Eve ate the fruit of evil and good into the body, the imagination of the body received vanity in the fruit. Now vanity awoke in the flesh, and the dark-world gained power and authority in the vanity of earthliness. At once, the beautiful, heavenly image that was from the being of the heavenly, divine world faded. Thus Adam and Eve died to the realm of heaven and awoke to the outer world. Then the beautiful soul faded with regard to the love of God, that is, in the holy strength and characteristic, and in its place awoke in the soul the fierce wrath, that is, the dark fire-world. The soul became in one part of the soul, namely in the inner nature, a half devil, and in the outer part of the outer world, a beast. Here is the purpose of death and the gate of hell, for which sake God became human, so that God might shatter death and transform hell once again into the great love, and destroy the vanity of the devil.

Let it be said to you, you human children: it has been said to you in the voice of the trumpet that you must go forth now from this shameful vanity, for the same fire burns.[18]

CHAPTER 3

Awakened Vanity

Now as Adam and Eve fell into this misery, then the fierceness of nature awoke in each characteristic, and in its desire imprinted into itself the vanity of earthliness and of the fierceness of God. Then the flesh became coarse and rough as of any other beast, and the noble soul became imprisoned thereby in the essence. And the soul looked at itself and saw that it had become a beast with regard to its body, and saw its bestial members for reproduction and the stinking maggot-sack in which the desire of the flesh could pack that which is vain.[19] They were ashamed of themselves before God and crawled off under the trees in the Garden of Eden.[20] Heat and cold also became noticeable to them.

Then heaven within the person shuddered at the horror.[21] Just as the earth shuddered in a rage when this wrath was shattered on

the cross with the sweetest love of God, so the wrath trembled before the great love of God.

And for the sake of this awakened vanity in the person, God
cursed the earth, so that the holy element would no longer press
through the outward fruit and bear fruit of paradise. For there was
no creature that could have taken nourishment from it.[22] Also, the
earthly person was no longer worthy of it. God did not want to cast
the noble pearls before beasts.[23] So an ungodly person in her or his
body is nothing other than a coarse, dumb beast. Although the person is a noble essence, the essence is completely poisoned and is
something loathsome before God.[24]

God's Promise: Love and Victory

Once God saw that God's beautiful image was spoiled, God revealed God's self before them and had mercy on them and promised
them the following as an eternal possession. In the humanity that
God would take on with God's greatest love, God would shatter the
serpent's characteristic, namely the characteristic of vanity in the
fierceness of God. God would break up violence with love. That was
the crushing of the head,[25] so that God would shatter dark death
and overcome anger with great love. God placed this covenant of
God's future incarnation into the light of life. In this covenant, the
Jewish sacrifices were directed toward a goal, because God had made
a promise to that goal with God's love. So the faith of the Jews went
to sacrifice, and God's imagination went into covenant. And the sacrifice was a prefiguring of the restoration of what Adam had lost.

Thus God reconciled God's wrath in the human characteristic
through the sacrifice in accordance with the goal of the covenant.
In this covenant the holiest name, Jesus, from the holy name and
great strength Jehovah, had embodied itself, because God wished
once again to move and to reveal God's own self in the being of the
heavenly world that faded in Adam, and to rekindle in it the holy
divine life.

Mary, the Covenant's Goal

The goal of this covenant was transmitted by Adam and his children from person to person, and spread from one to all, just as sin and the awakened vanity also spread from one to all. The goal was contained in the promise of the covenant, namely in the root of David, in Mary the Virgin. She was in the inner realm of the hidden humanity, namely the inner realm of the faded being in God's realm: she was the daughter of the covenant of God. And in the outer realm, in accordance with natural humanity, she was begotten by her rightful bodily father, Joachim, and her rightful mother, Anna, from their body essence and being and from their soul essence and being, like all of the children of Adam, a true a daughter of Eve.

In this Virgin Mary—in the promised goal of the covenant, of which all prophets had foretold—in the fulfillment of time, the eternally speaking word, which had created all things in accordance with its highest and deepest love and humility, moved in the name of Jesus. And this word introduced into the seed of Mary a living, divine, heavenly being into the humanity of the heavenly part that had faded with Adam, to which he had died in paradise. Understand that this being is in the transforming substance of love with regard to its characteristic, in which Adam should have reproduced himself in a magical, heavenly way, namely in the true woman's seed of heavenly being, which seed faded in paradise. As the divine light was extinguished in the same heavenly essence, God's word as the divine strength of divine understanding introduced heavenly, living being, and awakened the faded being in Mary's seed and brought it to life.[26]

The Heavenly Being Enters Humankind

And God's being, in which God dwells and operates, and the faded being of humankind, now became one person. Then the holy, divine being anointed the faded. Therefore this person is called Christ, an anointed of God.

And this is the withered rod of Aaron that sprouted and bore almonds,[27] and is that humanity of which Christ said in John 3:13 that he was to come from heaven and was in heaven, and so no one could come into heaven except the Son of man, who is from heaven. When he says, "He is come from heaven," he understands heavenly being,[28] heavenly corporeality. For the strength of God admits of no coming—it is everywhere, totally unmeasured and undivided. But being required a coming. The strength needed only to move itself and reveal itself in being.

The heavenly being, however, entered into the being that is human and took on that which is human, and not only the part of heavenly being that faded in Adam, but the complete human essence, in soul and flesh, according to all three worlds.

Here then lay our sickness and the death that Christ was to drown with the heavenly, holy blood. Christ took upon himself all our sin and sickness, likewise death and hell, in the fierceness of God, and shattered the realm of the devil in the human characteristic. The fierceness of God was the hell in which the Spirit of Christ entered, as Christ had now poured heavenly blood in our external human blood. He infused it with love and transformed that same hell in the human characteristic into heaven, and he led the human characteristic once again into equilibrium and restored it to the divine harmony.[29]

CHAPTER 4

Restoring the Inner, Heavenly Humanity

Here we now rightly understand our new birth: how we can be and remain a temple of God, and yet also be sinful, mortal people according to our outward humanity.[30] Christ has burst and opened in the human essence the gate of our inner, heavenly humanity that had been closed in Adam. And now it lies open to anyone, so that the soul might lead its will out from the vanity of the flesh, and lead it into this open gate in the Spirit of Christ.[31]

There must be a great, powerful earnestness—not only a learning and knowledge, but also a hunger and great thirst for Christ's Spirit. Knowledge alone is no faith. Rather, the hunger and thirst for what I desire, so that I imagine it and apprehend it and take it with the imagination: that is faith.

The will must leave the vanity of the flesh, yield itself willingly to the sufferings and death of Christ and to all the mockery of vanity,[32] and want no more of vanity but only desire the love of God in Christ Jesus.

And in such hunger and desire, the will imprints the person with the Spirit of Christ and with his heavenly corporeality; that is, the will's great hunger and thirst takes in the body of Christ, namely the heavenly being, within its faded image, in which image the word of the strength of God is the operative life.

The hunger of the soul leads its desire through the shattered characteristic of its humanity, which in Adam was faded with respect to its heavenly part. The sweet love-fire in the death of Christ shattered this characteristic when the death of the truly heavenly humanity was dashed into pieces. Then the hunger of the soul, through desire, grasped onto the holy, heavenly being, that is, the heavenly corporeality in its faded corporeality.[33] And thereby the faded, heavenly body rises in the strength of God, in the sweet name of Jesus.

And this awakened, heavenly, spiritual body is Christ's member and the temple of the Holy Spirit, a true dwelling of the Holy Trinity, as Christ promised, for he said, "We will come to you and make a dwelling in you" (2 Cor. 6:16). The same essence of the same life eats Christ's flesh and drinks his blood. Christ's Spirit, namely the word, made itself visible with the humanity of Christ, outside and within our faded humanity through the external person of the being of this world. This person eats Christ's holy being into his fiery being. Each spirit eats Christ's body.

Now when the soul eats of this sweet, holy, heavenly food, it enkindles itself in the great love in the name Jesus. Hence its fire of anguish becomes a great triumph and the true sun rises for it, in which it is born of another will. Here is the wedding of the Lamb. We heartily wish that the titular Christianity and jaw-Christianity might once experience this and pass from history into being.

Sophia, Heavenly Wisdom

But the soul does not receive the little pearl of holy power in the time of this life, because it still has as its possession the characteristic of the outward, bestial flesh in the outward person. The power of Christ, which in the wedding of the Lamb gets married, sinks into the image of heaven, namely into the being of the heavenly person, who is the temple of Christ. But that power does not sink into the fire-breath of the soul, which this entire time is at the outward realm, at the bond of vanity, and stands firmly bound to the air-breath, and is in great danger.

She indeed gives her love beams into the soul very often,[34] from which the soul receives its light. But the Spirit of Christ does not give itself at this time to the fire-breath, but only to the breath of the light that was extinguished in Adam. Therein is the temple of Christ, for it is the true, holy heaven.

So understand us rightly as to what the new birth is and how it happens. The outward, earthly, moral person is not reborn in this time, neither to the outward flesh nor the outward part of the soul. They both remain in the vanity of their will that was awakened in Adam. They love their mother, in whose body they live, namely the dominion of this outward world, and in it the birth of sin is revealed.

The outward person in soul and flesh—understand here the outward part of the soul—has no divine will and understands nothing of God. As the scripture says, "The natural person perceives nothing of the Spirit of God" (1 Cor. 2:14).

But the fire-breath of the inner world, once it is enlightened, understands God. It has a great groaning, hungering, and thirsting for the sweet little fountain of Christ. It refreshes itself through hungering and desiring, which is true faith, in the sweet fountain of Christ; with regard to its new body of heavenly being, it is like a hungering branch on the vine of Christ.

And that is the reason why the fiery soul cannot in this time come to perfection, because it stands bound fast to the outward bond of vanity, through which the devil constantly shoots his venomous beams upon the fiery soul and sifts it. As a result, it often bites the devil and poisons itself. From this arises great misery and anxiety, so that the noble Sophia hides in the little fountain of Christ in the heavenly humanity and cannot draw near to vanity.

For she knows how it went for her in Adam. Then she lost her little pearl, which from grace was given again to the inner humanity.[35]

Thus she faithfully calls to the fiery soul, as to her bridegroom, and exhorts the fiery soul to repentance and to unburdening or departing from the abomination of vanity. Then conflict commences in the whole person. Then the outward, fleshly person lusts against the inward, spiritual person, and the spiritual against the fleshly.[36] And the person stands in strife, full of affliction, worry, anxiety, and misery.

The Outward Soul of Reason

The inner person speaks to the fire-soul, "Oh, my faithless lover, turn around and depart from vanity, or you will lose my love and the noble little pearl." Thus speaks the outward reason, namely the bestial soul,[37] "You are foolish because you want to be the world's fool and scorn. You require the outer world for your life. Beauty, might, and splendor are the best thing for you. In them you can have joy. Why do you want to lead yourself into anxiety, misery, and scorn? Aspire to sensual pleasure that does well to the flesh and the soul's mind."

With such filth even a proper person is often soiled. The outer person soils himself or herself, just as a sow in the muck, and darkens his or her noble image. For the vainer the outer person becomes, the darker the inner person becomes, until the inner completely fades. So it happened by the beautiful little tree of paradise, and it will be difficult to acquire it again.

Then when the outward light, namely the outward soul, is once illumined, so that for the soul the outer light of reason is kindled through the inner light, the outer soul gives forth a hypocritical appearance and considers itself divine, even though the little pearl is gone.

So it is with many people, and therefore they often corrupt the pearl-tree in the little garden of Christ, concerning which the scripture predicts considerable difficulty: those who have once tasted the sweetness of the future world, if they fall from it again, will see the realm of God only with difficulty (Heb. 6:4–6).

And although it is so, that the gate of grace still stands open, the illusory light of the outward soul of reason keeps them away from it, because they think they have the little pearl, but they live only in the vanity of this world and dance with the devil according to his tune.[38]

CHAPTER 5

Real Christians, as Opposed to Christians in Name Only

Here Christians should reflect on why they call themselves Christian, and indeed should ponder if they are such. Although I may learn and understand that I am a sinner, that Christ put my sin to death on the cross and shed his blood for me—all this is far from making a Christian out of me. The inheritance belongs only to the children. A female servant in the house knows well what the woman of the house would like, but this does not make her the heir of the woman's goods. The devil also knows that there is one God,[39] but this does not make him an angel once again. But if the female servant in the house marries the son of the woman of the house, then she may indeed come into the inheritance of the woman's goods.

Our Christianity is to be understood similarly. It is not the children of history who are heirs of the goods of Christ, but rather legitimate children that have been reborn from Christ's Spirit. God said to Abraham, "Drive out the son of the female servant. He must not inherit with the son of the free woman" (Gal. 4:30). For he was a mocker and was only a son of history with regard to the faith and spirit of Abraham.[40] And so long as he was such, he was not in the true inheritance of the faith in Abraham. So God commanded Abraham to drive him out from his goods.

This was a prefiguring of the Christianity to come: the promise of Christianity took place in Abraham. Thus the figure was then shown in the two brothers, Isaac and Ishmael, as to how Christianity would behave; that there would be two kinds of people in it, true Christians and mouth-Christians, who under the name of Christianity would be mere mockers, like Ishmael. It was also shown through Esau, who was the image of the outward Adam, and Jacob, the image of Christ and of his true Christianity.

Therefore whoever wishes to be called a Christian ought to drive out the son of the servant, that is, the earthly, evil will, and always to kill and shatter the will, and to deny it the inheritance and not to give the little pearl to the bestial person for a plaything, so that the bestial person may constantly play around in the external light of the pleasure of the flesh. Instead, one should, with our father Abraham, lead the son of our true will to Mount Moriah, and in obedience offer it up to God,[41] always gladly willing to die to sin in Christ's death, to yield no rest in Christ's realm to the beast of vanity, not allowing one's self to become lascivious, arrogant, avaricious, envious, and malicious. These are the characteristics of Ishmael, the son of the servant, whom Adam sired in his vanity with the wanton prostitute, by the devil's imagination, from the earthly characteristic in the flesh.[42]

The mocker and titular Christian is a son of the prostitute, who must be driven out, for he must not inherit the legacy of Christ in the realm of God (Gal. 4:30). He is of no use and is only Babel, a confusion of the one language into many languages. He is only a babbler and a quarreler about the inheritance, and wants to chatter and quarrel about it with his mouth-hypocrisy and semblance of holiness. Yet he is only a bloodthirsty murderer of Abel his brother, who is a true heir.

Action, Not Mere Words

Therefore we tell it as we know it, that a person who wants to be called a Christian should test what kind of characteristics drive and govern him or her—whether the Spirit of Christ drives one to truth and righteousness and to the love of neighbor, so that one would eagerly do good, if one only knew how one could. And if one finds that one has a hunger for such virtue, then one may rightly consider that one is so drawn. Then one should direct the hunger into work, so as not simply to will and yet not act. The attraction of the Father to Christ consists in willing, but the true life consists in doing.

The right spirit acts rightly. But if there is a will to do and the doing does not follow, then the righteous person is in a vain pleasure that holds the doing captive and is only a hypocrite, an Ishmaelite. Such a person talks one thing and does another, and shows that one's mouth is a liar. What one teaches, one does not do oneself, and serves only the bestial person in vanity.

Someone may say, "I have the will and want eagerly to do good, but I have earthly flesh that constrains me, and I cannot. I shall, however, be saved by grace through the merits of the will of Christ. Indeed, because I console myself with Christ's suffering and merit, he will accept me through grace, thoroughly without merit on my part, and will forgive me my sins." Such a person acts like someone who knows what food is good for health and does not eat it, but instead eats poison from which they sicken and die.

What help is it to the soul if it knows the way to God but refuses to take it, and instead goes astray and does not reach God? What help is it to the soul if it takes consolation in being a child of Christ and in Christ's suffering and death, but itself plays the hypocrite and cannot enter into the childlike birth so that it can be born a true child from the Spirit of Christ, from Christ's suffering, death, and resurrection? Surely the flattery and hypocrisy concerning the merits of Christ, apart from the true, inwardly born child-state, is false and untrue, whoever teaches it.

This consolation belongs to the contrite sinner, who strives against sin and God's wrath when the temptations come with which the devil besets the soul. Then the soul must completely enwrap itself in the suffering and death of Christ, in Christ's merit.

Indeed Christ alone has merited it, but he has not earned it as a reward, as one who earns a wage, so that Christ gives us the child-state from his merit outwardly, and thus receives us into the child-state. No. Christ is himself the merit. He is the open gate through death, through whom we must enter. He does not, however, receive beasts into his merit, but rather those who convert and become as children.

These same children who come to Christ are Christ's wage. He has earned us. Therefore he also said, "Father, the people were yours, and you have given them to me, and I give them eternal life" (John 17:6). But the life of Christ will be given to no one unless one comes to him in the Spirit of Christ, into his humanity, suffering, and merit, and is born in his merit, a true child of merit. We must be born from his merit and put on the merit of Christ in his suffering and death. Not outwardly with mere mouth-hypocrisy, not only with consolation while remaining a foreign child of a foreign essence. No, the foreign essence does not inherit the child-state; rather the inwardly born essence inherits it.[43]

This inwardly born essence is not of this world but instead is in heaven. St. Paul says of it, "Our life is in heaven" (Phil. 3:20). The childlike essence lives in heaven, and heaven is in the person. But if heaven is not open in the person, and one only stands hypocritically before heaven and says, "I am indeed outside, but Christ wants to receive me through grace; his merit is indeed mine," such a person is according to the outward person in vanity and sin, and with the soul in hell, that is, in God's wrath.

Therefore learn to understand truly what Christ has taught and done for us. He is our heaven and must gain a form in us,[44] if we are to be in heaven. Thus the inner soul-person is with the holy body of Christ, that is, in the new birth, in heaven, and the outer, mortal person is in the world. Concerning this, Christ said, "My little sheep are in my hand; no one can tear them away from me. The Father, who has given them to me, is greater than everything" (John 10:27–29).

CHAPTER 6

The Stone Church of Babel and the Inward Church of Saints

Dear brothers and sisters, we wish to speak with you faithfully, not from a hypocritical mouth to please the Antichrist, but from our little pearl, from Christlike essence and knowledge; not from husk and history, but from a childlike spirit and knowledge of Christ, as a branch on the vine Christ, from the measure of the knowledge revealed to us in God's counsel.

One binds us now to the history, to stone churches, which in their worth would in fact be good, if one also brought the temple of Christ into them.

One teaches that the churches' absolution is a forgiveness of sins. Likewise it is taught that the Lord's Supper takes away sin. Again it is taught that the Spirit of God is poured forth through the office of preaching.

All this would have its way if it were correctly explained and if one did not cling to the husk.[45] Many go to church twenty or thirty years, hear sermons, and make use of the sacraments, let themselves be absolved, and are just as much a beast of the devil as the next person.[46] A beast goes to the churches and to communion, and a beast goes out again. How does one who has no mouth wish to eat? How does one who has no hearing wish to hear? Also can one enjoy food whose mouth is shut tight? How does one wish to drink who is far from water? What help is it to me, that I go into the wall-church and fill my ears with an empty breath? Or go to the Lord's Supper and feed only the earthly mouth that is mortal and perishable? Can I not just as well give the earthly mouth a piece of bread at home, so that it is satisfied? What help is it to the soul, which is an immortal life, that the bestial person observes the form of the practice of Christ but the soul cannot attain to the treasure of the practice? For St. Paul says, concerning the Lord's Supper, "Because you do not discern the body of the Lord, you receive it to your own judgment" (1 Cor. 11:29).

The covenant endures; it was moved in practice. Christ offers us Christ's Spirit in his word, that is, in the preached word, his body and blood in the sacraments, and his absolution in fraternal and sororal reconciliation.[47]

What help is it, however, if a beast listens but has no hearing of the inner, living word, and no vessel in which it can lay the word so that it may bring forth fruit? Concerning these matters Christ says, "The devil rips the word from their hearts, so that they may not believe and be saved" (Luke 8:12). Why? Because the word finds no place where it may take hold in the hearing.

Likewise with absolution: what help is it that someone says to me, "I proclaim to you the absolution of your sins," but the soul remains totally locked up in sin? Whoever says this to a locked-up sinner is mistaken, and the one who receives this without God's voice within is also self-deceived.

No one can forgive sin except God alone. The preacher's mouth does not have forgiveness in its own power. The Spirit of Christ has forgiveness in the voice of the priest's mouth, if the priest is also a Christian. But what help was that to those who heard Christ teach on earth when he said, "Come to me all you who are weary and heavy-laden, and I will revive you"? What help was it to those who heard it but were not weary? Where was the reviving? Since they had dead ears and only heard the outward Christ but not the word of divine power, they were not revived. A hypocritical absolution is no more helpful to a bestial person; the same with the sacraments.

It is now as clear regarding sacraments as it is regarding the office of teaching. The covenant is moved. The feeding of the soul takes place, but according to the characteristic of the mouth of the soul. That is, the external beast receives bread and wine, which it could just as well eat at home. The fiery soul receives the testament in accordance with its characteristic,[48] that is, in the wrath of God. It receives the being of the eternal world, but in accordance with the characteristic of the dark-world. As the mouth is, so also is the food that belongs in the mouth. The mouth receives the food as judgment upon itself, in the way that the godless will see Christ at the Last Judgment, as a severe, harsh judge. The saints will see Christ as a dear Emmanuel.

Toward the godless, God's wrath stands clear in God's testament, and toward the saints, the heavenly corporeality stands clear, and in it the power of Christ in the holy name Jesus. But what help is the holy to the godless if they cannot benefit from it? What is supposed to take away the sin of the godless? Sin is only stirred up and is revealed.

For the saints, however, there is no remission of sins in the sacraments, nor forgiveness through them. Instead, it is like this: When Christ rises, Adam dies in the essence of the serpent. When the sun comes up, night is swallowed up in day and is no longer night. Thus is the forgiveness of sins. The Spirit of Christ eats of Christ's holy being. The inner person is the setting of holy being and receives what the Spirit of Christ brings into it as the temple of God: Christ's flesh and blood. What about the beast? Or what about the devil, or the soul in God's wrath? They eat of their heavenly body in which they dwell, namely in the abyss.

Likewise with the office of preaching: the godless hears what the outer soul preaches to the outer world and takes it in as a history. If however there is stubble or straw in the sermon, the godless sucks the vanity out of it, and the soul sucks false poison and the devil's murder out of it. With this the soul tickles its fancy because it hears how it can direct people. If the preacher is also a dead one and sows poison and outrage from a troubled state, then the devil teaches and the devil hears. This same teaching is caught in the godless heart and bears godless fruit. From this the world has become a murderous pit of the devil, so that both in teacher and listener there is nothing within but vain mockery, slander, sneering, quarrels about words, and biting about the husks.[49]

But in the holy teacher the Holy Spirit teaches, and in the holy listener the Spirit of Christ hears through the soul and the divine container of the divine sound. The saints have their church within, where they hear and teach inwardly. Babel, on the other hand, has a stone heap where it enters to dissemble and dazzle. Babel lets itself be seen with beautiful clothes and poses itself as devout and pious. The stone church is its god in which it places its confidence.

The saints, on the other hand, have their church within and with them in every place. For the saints stand and move, lie and sit, in their church. The saints are in the true Christian church, in the temple of Christ. The Holy Spirit preaches to the saints from all creatures. In all that the saints look at, they see a preacher of God.

Here the mocker will say that I disdain the stone church where the congregation gathers. To this I say, "No." Rather, I point to the hypocritical Whore of Babylon, who carries on her whoring with the stone church and calls herself a Christian but is a wretch of a whore.[50]

True Christians bring along their holy church into the congregation. Their heart is the true church where they should cultivate worship. If I were to go to church for a thousand years and to the sacrament each week and also to let myself be absolved each and every day, but if I did not have Christ in me, it would all be false and a useless trifle, a carved idol in Babel. It is not a forgiveness of sins.

The saints do holy works, from the holy power of their soul's mind. The work is not the reconciliation, but it is the building that the true Spirit builds in the spirit's being. It is the saints' dwelling place, just as the fiction of the false Christians is their dwelling place, where their souls go in hypocrisy. The outer hearing goes into what is external and works in the external, and the inner hearing goes into what is internal and works in the internal.

Play the hypocrite, howl, cry, sing, preach, teach as you will. If the inner teacher and hearer is not open, it is all Babel and fiction and a carved idol, where the spirit of the outer world makes a model or idol in imitation of the inner. With the idol this spirit dazzles, as though it had a holy worship-service. At times, however, the devil works mightily in the imagination in the midst of such a service, and indeed titillates the heart with such things that the flesh likes to have. This even occurs often with respect to the outward humanity, to the children of God. If they are not watchful of themselves, the devil sifts with them.

CHAPTER 7

Genuine Christians Do Not Quarrel about Religion

Genuine people who are reborn in Christ's Spirit are in the simplicity of Christ and have no quarrel with anyone about religion. They have enough interior strife with the bestial, evil, flesh and blood. They consider themselves great sinners and fear God, for their sins stand manifest and are under judgment. For the chaos locks the sins within itself. The wrath of God reproaches the people as guilty in their own eyes. But the love of Christ presses through and drives out the chaos, as day swallows night.

For the godless, however, their sins rest in the sleep of death and sprout forth in the abyss and bring forth fruits in hell.

The Christianity in Babel quarrels about knowledge: how one should serve, honor, and know God; what God is according to God's being and willing. They teach poorly that whoever is not united with them on all points in knowledge and opinion is not Christian, but rather a heretic.

Now I would gladly like to see how one should bring all their sects together into one that could call itself the Christian church, because they are altogether merely despisers. Each heap of them slanders the others and decries them as false.

Christians, however, have no sect. They can dwell in the midst of the sects, even appear in their worship services and yet cling to no sect. They have only a single knowledge, which is Christ within. They seek only one path, which is the desire that they always want to act and to live rightly. They place all knowing and willing in the life of Christ. They sigh and wish always that only God's will be done within themselves, and that God's realm may become revealed within. Daily and hourly they kill the sins in the flesh. For the seed of the woman, as the inner person in Christ, constantly tramples the head of the devil in vanity (Gen. 3:15).

The Christians' faith is a desire toward God that they have wrapped up in the sure hope, in which one risks all for words of the promise. They live and die in the hope, and yet never die with regard to the real person. For Christ also said thus, "Whoever believes in me will never die but has pressed through from death to life." Again, "There will be streams of living water flowing from her or him," as good teachings and works.[51]

Therefore I say that all is Babel that bites and quarrels with one another over the letter. The letters stand all in one root, which is the Spirit of God, just as the various flowers all stand in the earth and all grow next to one another. None bites the other because of color, scent, or taste. They permit the sun, along with rain and wind and heat and cold, to do with them as they wish, yet each one grows in its essence and characteristic. So it is also with the children of God. They have various gifts and knowledge, but are all from one Spirit. They rejoice with one another in the great miracles of God and thank the Most High in God's wisdom. Why should they quarrel about the One in whom they live and are, and of whose being they themselves are?

It is the greatest foolishness in Babel that the devil has made the world quarrel about religion, so that they quarrel about self-made opinions, about the letter. The realm of God, however, is not in any opinion, but rather in power and in love. Christ also said, and ultimately left it with his disciples: they should love one another. In this way everyone would recognize that they were his disciples, just as he loved them.[52] If people aspired to love and righteousness as they do for opinions, there would be no contention at all on earth. We would live as children in our Father and would no longer need law or statutes.

For God is not served by any law, but only by obedience. Laws are on account of the wicked, who do not want love and righteousness and who are driven and compelled by laws. We all have one single statute: that we still ourselves before the Lord of all being, and yield our will to God and allow God's Spirit to work in us, to play and to do as God wills. And we return to God, as God's fruit, what God works and reveals in us.

So now if we do not quarrel about the various fruits, gifts, and knowledge, but instead recognize one another as children of God, who would judge us? The realm of God does not lie in our knowing and presuming, rather in power.

If we did not know half so much and were more childlike and had only a fraternal and sororal will toward one another and lived as children of one mother, like the branches of a tree that all take sap from one root, we would be much more holy.

Knowledge is only for the purpose that we learn it because we have lost the divine power in Adam and are now inclined toward evil,[53] so that we learn to recognize how we have evil characteristics in us and that doing evil does not please God. Thereby with this knowledge we learn to act rightly. Insofar as we have the power of God in us and desire with all powers to do and to live rightly, knowledge is only our play, in which we enjoy ourselves.

For the true knowing is the revelation of the Spirit of God through eternal wisdom. God knows what God wants in God's children. God pours out wisdom and miracles through God's children, just as the earth pours forth the various flowers. If we now dwell next to one another in Christ's Spirit as humble children, and each one rejoices in the gifts and knowledge of the other, who would judge us? Who judges the birds in the forest that praise the Lord of all being with various voices, each from its essence? Does God's Spirit punish them for not bringing their voices into one harmony? Indeed, all sound originates from God's power, and they play before God.

Therefore the people that quarrel concerning knowledge and God's will, and therefore disdain one another, are more foolish than the birds in the forest and the wild beasts that have no true understanding. They are less useful before God than the flowers of the field that keep silent before the Spirit of God, and allow God to reveal divine wisdom and power through them. Indeed, they are worse than the thistles and thorns among the beautiful flowers that keep silent. They are like predatory beasts and birds in the forest that frighten away the other birds from their singing and praise of God.

In sum, they are the devil's growth in the wrath of God, which through their pain must nevertheless serve the Lord. For with their vexation and persecution they drive out the sap through the essence of the children of God, so that the children of God move themselves in the Spirit of God with prayer and diligent supplication, in which the Spirit of God moves itself in them. For the desire is exerted through this, and also through the children of God, so that they sprout and bear fruit.[54] For in tribulation God's children are revealed, according to the scripture: when you chastise them, they cry to you in anguish.[55]

CHAPTER 8

The Sum of Christian Religion: Returning to Unity

The whole Christian religion consists in this: that we learn to know what we are; whence we have come; how we have gone out of unity and entered into disunity, evil, and unrighteousness; how we have awakened the foregoing in ourselves. Next: where we were in the unity since we were children of God. Third: how we are now in disunity, in conflict and antipathy. Fourth: where we go forth out of this fragile life;[56] where we should want to go forth with the immortal, and then also where with the mortal.

In these four points consists what is to be learned about our whole religion: how to come out of disunity and vanity, and to enter again into one tree out of which we all have come in Adam, which tree is Christ in us. We must not dispute about anything nor have any conflict. Let each exert him- or herself to be able to enter once again into the love of God and of one's brothers and sisters.

Christ's testaments are absolutely nothing other than a brotherly and sisterly bond by which God is bound with us in Christ, and we with God. All teaching should be directed to this, as well as all willing, living, and doing. Whatever teaches or does otherwise is Babel and fable, only an idol of arrogance, a useless judgment, a going astray of the world, a devilish glitter with which the devil masks simplicity.

All Is to Be Done in God's Spirit

Whatever some people teach outside of God's Spirit, and whoever has no understanding and nevertheless sets oneself up as a teacher in the realm of God and wants to serve God by teaching, is false. Such a people serve only the idol of their belly and their proud haughty mind, because they want to be honored and want to be called holy. They bear an office chosen by human children but only pose as saints, and they have set them in office only for the sake of favor. Christ said that whoever does not enter the sheep pen by the door, that is, through him, but climbs in some other way, is a thief and a murderer, and the sheep do not follow him for they do not know his voice (John 10:5).

They do not have the voice of the Spirit of God, but only the voice of their skill and learning. They instruct not God's Spirit. But Christ says, "All plants that my heavenly Father has not planted will be uprooted" (Matt. 15:13). How will the godless then plant heavenly plants when their power has no seed within it? Christ plainly says, "The sheep do not hear his voice; they do not follow him" (John 10:5).[57] The written word is only a tool with which the Spirit leads.

The word that wishes to teach must be alive in the word that is written with letters. The Spirit of God must be in the resonance of the letters. Otherwise no one is a teacher of God but is only a teacher of the letter, a knower of history but not of the Spirit of God in Christ. All that with which one wishes to serve God must happen in faith, that is, in the spirit that makes the work complete and acceptable to God. What a person begins and performs in faith is done in the Spirit of God who cooperates in the work. That is acceptable to God, for God's own self has done it, and God's power is in it. It is holy.

But what is done in the self without faith is only a shadow or husk of a true Christian work.

If you serve your brother or sister and do it only for show and give it grudgingly, you do not serve God. For your faith does not originate in love and does not proceed into the hope that is in your gift. Indeed, you serve, and your brother or sister thanks God and also blesses you. But you do not bless him or her since you give with a murmuring spirit in your gift, which does not enter into God's Spirit in the hope of faith. Therefore your gift is only half-given, and you have only half the reward for it.

Receiving is to be understood similarly. If one gives in faith in divine hope, one blesses one's gifts in one's faith. But one who receives them ungratefully and grumbles in spirit curses them in the enjoyment. Therefore each one gets one's own due. What one sows one also reaps.

Thus also in the office of teaching. What one sows one also reaps. If one sows good seed from Christ's Spirit, it adheres in the good heart and bears good fruit. But in the godless who are not receptive, the wrath of God is stirred up. If one sows quarreling, disdaining, and slandering, then all godless people receive that. It also adheres and bears such fruit that one mocks, scoffs at, defames, and slanders one another.

Out of this the great Babel is born and grows. When people quarrel out of haughtiness over the history of the justification of the poor sinner before God, they cause the simple to go astray and to become slanderous so that one brother or sister scorns the other for the sake of the history and the changing of letters, and consigns him or her to the devil.[58]

Such slanderous wretches do not serve God but rather the great edifice of disunity. Because a corrupt plague lies in all people in the earthly flesh, they awaken abomination even in the simple children of God, and make the people of God, along with the children of iniquity, become slanderous. And the wretches are only master builders of the great Babel and of the world, and are just as useful as the fifth wheel of a wagon, not to mention that they raise the hellish structure.

Depart from Dispute and Disunity

Therefore it is highly necessary for the children of God to pray earnestly and to learn to recognize this false structure, to depart from it with their soul's mind, and also not to help build it, or to persecute the children of God themselves and thereby keep themselves out of the realm of God and be led astray. As Christ said to the Pharisees, "Woe unto you, Pharisees. You travel over land and sea to make a convert, and when he or she has become one, you make him or her a child of hell, twice as much as you are" (Matt. 23:15). The same thing truly happens in the current rabble and sects with the criers and teachers of quarreling.

Therefore all children of God who consider themselves members of Christ must depart from such horrible disputing and blood duels—concerning which the gifts revealed to me from God have faithfully warned—and quarrels with brothers and sisters, and simply aspire for love and righteousness toward all people.

For if one is a good tree, then one should also bear good fruit. Although one must sometimes permit that swine eat one's fruit, one should nonetheless remain a good tree and constantly want to work with God and not let any evil overcome oneself. Thus one stands in God's field and bears fruit for God's table, which one shall enjoy eternally. Amen.

The End.

3

TRUE YIELDEDNESS

J AKOB BOEHME composed this treatise in 1622. It was published the following year along with another short work, *True Repentance*. After Boehme's death, nine of his short works were gathered and published under the title *The Way to Christ*, and *True Yieldedness* was among them.

The word *Gelassenheit* in the title, here rendered as "yieldedness," has a long history as a bedrock term in the German mystical tradition, and contains numerous layers of meaning. Among them are concepts of submission, resignation, relinquishing one's own will, and releasing. To use the phrase of contemporary twelve-step programs, *Gelassenheit* means "Let go and let God." The word also carries overtones of tranquillity, serenity, and equanimity.

The fourteenth-century Dominican mystic Johannes Tauler, who was widely read among Boehme's contemporaries, describes *Gelassenheit* in his second sermon on Pentecost. For Tauler, *Gelassenheit* entails leaving behind everything, even one's hope of enjoying the presence of God, in order to conform one's will to the will of God:

A person is completely stripped of one's self in complete and genuine resignation to God. One sinks deeply into the ground of the divine will, to linger in this poverty and nakedness, not for a week or a month, but rather, if God wills, for a thousand years or a full eternity. Or if God were to wish to have one forever in hellfire, in eternal pain, so that one could thoroughly yield oneself therein, children, that would be true *Gelassenheit* ... with this *Gelassenheit* one sets one's foot truly into eternal life, and after this pain one never again comes into another, neither into hell nor into any other suffering, and it is impossible that God would ever forsake this person.[1]

This mystical tradition of utter abandonment to the will of God underpins Boehme's thoughts on *Gelassenheit*.

For Jakob Boehme, a fundamental problem for human beings is possessiveness. Possessiveness manifests the human desire to dominate and to control more than is really in our power, and more than God has put at our disposal. Domination leads us into the world of wrath rather than the world of love. It brings strife and conflict, as Boehme saw so clearly in the Thirty Years' War that raged around him. The lust for dominion expresses itself in arrogance. Most people are not princes fighting over earthly territory, but we are all tempted by arrogance inwardly, through our misuse of reason and knowledge. Both reason and knowledge are great gifts from God, but they are to be held lightly, not possessively.

As Boehme sees it, you are what you eat—and you eat what you are. God's intent for humankind was to eat of the fruit of paradise in that primordial state of harmony and balance that prevailed before the Fall, when good and evil were revealed. Adam and Eve, however, rebelled and chose instead "to eat from the characteristic of the self, that is, from the dominion of life in which good and evil stand." Motivated by selfish desire, they departed from yieldedness. According to Boehme, humans (and angels) have great powers of self-determination. By orienting our will, we can choose to live in the world of fire and wrath, or the world of light and love.

Each of these worlds arises from a center or matrix that shapes the quality of what originates from it, for good or evil. In this essay, Boehme frequently uses the word *Mutter*, usually translated as "mother," though it can also mean "matrix." In alchemy, *Mutter* or "matrix" could mean a kind of vessel as well as a base metal—each of them a place of origin. Finally, *Mutter* can mean "womb." All these should be borne in mind when encountering the word "mother" or "matrix" in Jakob Boehme.

Another term that occurs with some frequency in this treatise is *Kindschaft*, usually translated here as the "child-state," referring to a filial relationship with God, which humans can return to through the new birth. Boehme may intend the reader to hear an echo of the apostle Paul in his epistles to the Galatians (Gal. 4:5) and to the Romans (Rom. 8:23 and 9:4), where Paul speaks of being adopted into a filial relationship in the household of faith. In Luther's translation of the Bible that Boehme read, the word used to describe this adoption is *Kindschaft*.

The spiritual method that Boehme proposes here is similar to that in his other writings, especially *Life Beyond the Senses*. One is to cast away one's thoughts, to wish to desire nothing and to learn nothing, and to sink into love, grace, and humility. The soul's mind is to wrap itself in Christ's death, inwardly to die and rise with Christ. This sinking into oneself and into divine love is the heart of yieldedness. In addition to this language of wrapping, Boehme uses his common expression of "pressing":

> One's own desire presses into the nothing, only into the doing and acting of God that God wishes in it; and the Spirit of God presses out through the desire of yielded humility. Thus the human self looks to the Spirit of God who sees everything that is in time and eternity, because everything is near to it.

Finally, another theme familiar from other writings of Boehme is his challenge to the hypocrisy of the institutional church whose members claim, on the basis of the historical event of Christ's death, to be forgiven for their sins while they continue to lead an immoral life. For Boehme, this is only "history," and personal experience is essential for the inward life. Boehme often calls this hypocritical institution the Babel Church, referring to the Tower of Babel, where the original, pure human language was confused through human pride, creating divisions among people in Genesis 11. In Boehme's German, "Babel" is also the same word for "Babylon," and so his use of "Babel" echoes the notorious beast of Babylon in Revelation 17.

In short, in *True Yieldedness* Jakob Boehme draws on the traditions of scripture and mysticism to articulate his conception of the basic human problem as selfish departure from God's will. To sink into yieldedness is to open the way to return to God and to the primordial human state before the Fall in Eden.

TRUE YIELDEDNESS

BOOK I

The Problem of Possessiveness

In Lucifer as also in Adam, the first person, we have a true model of what the self does when it appropriates outward light as its own possession so that the self can live in its own dominion in the understanding. One also sees this in well-educated people: when they acquire the light of outward nature as a possession in their own reason, nothing but arrogance arises from it. Yet all the world fervently seeks and desires it as the best treasure. And indeed it is the best treasure of this world, if it were used rightly.

Arrogantly Shining the Light of Reason into the Self

But because the self, namely reason, is captive and remains tightly bound in this strong prison, that is, God's wrath, as well as in earthliness, it is truly dangerous for a person if one introduces the light of knowledge into the self, as a possession of the self.

For the fierceness of the eternal and temporal nature soon takes pleasure in it. From this the self and its own reason rise up in arrogance and break away from true, yielded humility toward God and no longer wish to eat of the fruit of paradise, but instead they wish to eat from the characteristic of the self, that is, from the dominion of life in which good and evil stand, just as Lucifer and Adam did. Both of them, with the desire of the creaturely self, entered again into the original condition out of which creatures are brought forth and proceed as a creature—Lucifer went into the center of fierce nature, into the matrix of the fire, and Adam into the earthly nature, into the matrix of the outer world, namely into the longing for evil and good.

This happened to both of them because they shined the light of reason in the self, in which they could mirror themselves and behold themselves in being. By this means, the spirit of the self entered into the imagination, that is, into a desire for a center in order to exalt itself and to become great and mighty and thereby more wise.[2] As Lucifer sought the mother of fire in his center, and thereby thought to rule over God's love of God and all the angelic host, Adam also desired to test the mother, out of which evil and good flow in the essence. There Adam led his desire, into the will, thereby to become wise and intelligent.

Captive to Desire

Both Lucifer and Adam were captive in their false desires, in the mother, and they broke away from the yieldedness to God and were captured by the spirit of the will, by the spirit of the mother. Desire presently obtained dominion in the creature. Consequently Lucifer remained in the fierce, dark fire-quality, and the same fire was revealed in the spirit of his will, through which the creature in the desire became an enemy of the love and gentleness of God.

Revelation of Opposition

So Adam was also immediately seized by the earthly mother that is evil and good, created out of God's love and wrath into one being. Immediately the earthly characteristic obtained dominion in Adam. From this it happened that heat and cold, envy, wrath, and all false antipathy and evil against God were revealed and governed in him.

But if they had not directed the light of knowledge into the self, then the mirror of the knowledge of the center and the original condition of the creature, out of which the imagination and longing arise, would not have been revealed.

Reason and Will Are Still Temptations, Leading to Arrogance

To a certain measure, this still brings danger to the enlightened children of God today, such that when the sun of the great appearance of God's holiness shines upon many, by which the life advances into triumph, reason mirrors itself in it. And the will enters into the self, namely into its own search, and wishes to test the center, out of which the light shines, and to force itself into the self.

From this arises the miserable arrogance and one's own darkness, so that one's own reason thinks itself to be something more.[3] Reason thinks that though it does what it wishes, God's will is operative through it. Reason thinks that it is a prophet. And yet it is only in itself and moves in its own desire, in which the center of the creature swings itself immediately into the height and enters with its own desire of falsehood against God, so that the will enters into a darkness.

Then the flattering devil steps up to the person and sifts the center of the creature and brings the devil's false desires into the center, so that the person becomes as though drunk in one's self and becomes persuaded that one is driven by God. In this way the good beginning, in which the light of God became shining in the creature, is corrupted, and the same light of God fades from the person.

Mistaking Outward Light for Inward

Then the outward light of the outward nature remains shining in the creature, for one's own self swings into the outward light, so the self then thinks that it is still the first light from God. But no, in this the devil swings himself in once again with his sevenfold desire,[4] after he has had to fade in the first light, which is divine. Of this Christ says, "When the unclean spirit departs from a person, it wanders through dry places and seeks rest and does not find it. Then it takes to itself seven spirits that are worse than it, and returns once more into its first house and finds it swept with brooms and adorned, and dwells there. Then it is worse with the person than it was before" (Matt. 12:43, 45).

Swinging the Light of Reason to the Center

This adorned house is the light of reason in the self. For then the same love appears to one with its very friendly appearance, through which the outward light of reason is enkindled. For where God's light enkindles itself, all becomes light. Then the devil cannot stay; he must depart from there. So he searches thoroughly for the mother of the primordial condition of life, that is, the center. But it has become a dry, powerless place. The wrath of God, that is, the center of nature, is in its own characteristic totally impotent, sterile, and dry, and cannot come to dominion. Satan examines this place to learn if he can find any gate open, where he can turn in with desire and sift the soul, so that it may exalt itself.

Delusion, False Imaginations, Drunkenness

And if the spirit of the will of the creature swings with the light of reason into the center, that is, into the self, and enters into its own delusion, then it departs again from God's light. Now the devil finds himself an open gate and a beautifully adorned house as his dwelling, namely the light of reason. So he takes to himself the seven forms of the characteristics of life in the self, that is, the hypocrites that have gone out from God and into the self. Then he turns in and sets his desires and false imagination into the longing of the self. When the spirit of the will sees itself in the forms of the life-characteristics in the outward life, then it sinks into itself, as if it were drunk. Then the stars seize it and direct their mighty stars into it, to seek there the miracles of God and to reveal themselves in them. For all creation yearns for God. And though the stars cannot seize the Spirit of God, yet they would much rather have a house of light in which they can find pleasure than a locked house that is of no help.

Thus this person continues, as if drunk by means of the stars. This person grasps great, wondrous things, and has a constant leader in the stars. Then the devil notes keenly where a gate stands open for him, where he can enkindle the center of life, so that the spirit of the will may ascend into the heights, in its own arrogance, in its darkness.[5]

The Will of Reason Desires Honor

From this arises the will's own honor, in that the will of reason wishes to be honored. For the will thinks that it has the prize of salvation because it has the light of reason and can put the locked-up house in order, which however God can indeed unlock. The will thinks it is now due the honor because it has attained to the understanding of reason. It never realizes how the devil amuses himself with his desire in the seven life-forms of the center of nature. The will never realizes what an abominable error it has made.

False Babel in the Church

From this understanding the false Babel is brought forth in the Christian church on earth. There one directs and governs by the conclusions of reason. There one sets over the church the child of drunkenness—very finely adorned with its self and its own desire—as a beautiful virgin.

But the devil has moved into the seven life-forms of the center as a lodging, that is, into the self of his own reason, and constantly directs his will and desire into this adorned virgin whom the stars have received into their service. He is her beast, upon which she royally rides forth, as finely adorned in her own life-forms.[6] Thus she has taken in the outward radiance from God's holiness, namely the light of reason, and supposes that she is a beautiful child in the house, for the devil is at home within her.

Thus it is for all who once were enlightened by God and departed from true yieldedness and weaned themselves from the true mother breast, namely proper humility.

How the Process of a True Christian Takes Place

Reason orders me to stop and says, "It is indeed right and good that a person attain the light of God as well as the light of outward nature and reason, in order that one might govern one's life wisely, according to holy scripture."[7]

Used Rightly, Reason Is Good

Yes, it is right, and nothing can be more useful, and nothing better can happen to a person. It is a treasure above all treasures of this world, for whoever can attain to and receive the light of time, since it is an eye of time and eternity.

But hear how you ought to use it. The light of God first reveals itself in the soul. It shines forth like a light from a candle and at once enkindles the outward light of reason, but not so that it might completely hand itself over to reason, that is, to the outward person's dominion. No, the outward person perceives oneself in the penetrating brilliance, as an image before a mirror. Thereupon one learns to know oneself in the self, which is good and useful for the person.

Now when this takes place, the reason, that is, the creaturely self, can do nothing better than not to contemplate itself in the creaturely self, and not to enter the center with the will of desire and search for itself. Otherwise reason breaks itself off from God's being,[8] and eats of the outward light and being, through which reason again draws poison into itself.

Sinking into Love

The will of the creature should, with all reason and desire, totally sink into itself, like an unworthy child that is indeed not worthy of this high grace. It should not allocate to itself any knowledge or understanding, nor should it request or desire from God any understanding in the creaturely self. Instead, it should only sink itself plainly and simply into the love and grace of God in Christ Jesus, and desire to be as though dead to its reason and self in the life of God, and to submit itself fully to the life of God in love, so that God might do with it how and what God wishes, as God's tool.

One's own reason should not busy itself with any speculations on divine or human basis. Reason should also not wish or desire anything except God's grace in Christ alone. Just as a child longs only for its mother's breast, so should reason's hunger constantly enter into God's love and not allow itself to be broken away from that hunger by anything. When the outward reason triumphs in the light and says, "I have the true child," then the will of desire should bend reason to earth and direct it into the deepest humility and simple unknowing, and say to it, "You are foolish and have nothing but God's grace. You must entwine yourself in this with great humility and be completely as nothing within yourself. You neither know nor love yourself." All that is on or in you must regard and consider itself as worthless except as a mere tool of God, and must direct its desire into God's mercy alone. All that is on or in you must also depart from all self-knowing and willing, to consider them also as worthless, and to conceive no will to enter into them again in the near or distant future.

When this takes place, the natural will becomes powerless, and the devil can no longer sift it with his false desire. For the place of his rest becomes completely dry and powerless.

Enkindling the Flame of Love

Then the Holy Spirit receives the life-forms from God and takes command. That is, the Holy Spirit enkindles the life-forms with the flame of love. And then arises the high learning and knowledge of the center of all being, in accordance with the inner and outer stars of the creature, in a very subtle, driving fire, with great desire, to sink itself into the same light and thereby to consider itself unworthy and worthless.

Thus one's own desire presses into the nothing, that is, only into the doing and acting of God that God wishes in it; and the Spirit of God presses out through the desire of yielded humility. Thus the human self looks to the Spirit of God in the trembling and joy of humility. And so it may see everything that is in time and eternity. Everything is near to it.

When the Spirit of God rises like a fire in the flame of love, then the spirit of the will of the soul submits itself and says, "Lord, may the honor be to your name and not to me. You have the might to take power, might, strength, wisdom, and knowledge. Do what you will. I can no longer know anything. I wish to go nowhere unless you lead me as your tool. Do in me and with me what you wish."

In such a humble, complete submission, the spark of divine power falls like tinder into the center of the life-forms, namely into the soul-fire, which Adam had made into a dark coal, and the spark glimmers. And when the light of divine power has enkindled itself in it, then the creature must proceed as a tool of the Spirit of God and speak what the Spirit of God says, because the creature is no longer its own possession but rather is the tool of God.

But in this fiery, driving force, the will of the soul must ceaselessly sink itself into the nothing, namely into the deepest humility before God. As soon as it wishes to go the least bit in its own examination, the devil reaches it in the center of the life-forms and sifts it so that it goes into the self. For it must remain in yielded humility, just as a spring from its source, and must ceaselessly draw from and drink from God's fountain and in no way desire to depart from God's way.

Eating of the Self

For as soon as the soul eats of the self and of the light of reason, then it strays into its own delusion. Then the thing that the soul takes for something divine is only the outward constellation, which as soon as it seizes the soul makes the soul drunk. Then the soul runs into error until it fully submits itself once more into yieldedness and acknowledges itself anew as a soiled child, and dies once more to reason and attains to God's love again. This happens with greater difficulty than it did the first time, for the devil vigorously brings in doubt. He does not willingly leave his robber castle.[9]

One sees this clearly in the saints of God from throughout the world until now. How many were moved by the Spirit of God, and yet at times departed out of yieldedness and entered into the self, that is, into their own reason and willing, in which Satan threw them down into sin and God's wrath. This can be seen in David and Solomon, as well as in the ancestors and apostles, in that they at times committed powerful errors, when they went out of yieldedness and entered into the self, namely into their own reason and the desire of reason.

Desire and Learn Nothing

Therefore it is necessary for the children of God to know what they are to do with themselves if they wish to learn the way of God. They must shatter and cast away their thoughts, and wish to desire nothing and to learn nothing. Then they will experience themselves in true yieldedness. They will experience that God's Spirit teaches, leads, and directs the human spirit, and that the human will for its own desire is completely broken and submitted to God.

All speculating about the wonders of God is almost a dangerous thing with which the spirit of the will can easily be captivated. Only if the spirit of the will attends to the Spirit of God does it have the power in yielded humility to see all the wonders of God.

I am not saying that a person is to seek and learn nothing in the natural arts. No, for this is useful to reason. But one's own reason is not to be the starting place. One should direct one's life not only through the light of outward reason, which is indeed good, but a person is to sink with that light into the deepest humility before God, set the Spirit and will of God foremost in all one's searching, so that the light of reason might see through God's light. And though reason knows much, it must not however assume this to itself as its own possession, but rather give the honor to God, to whom alone is knowledge and wisdom.

Humility Leads to the Highest Knowledge

For the more reason sinks itself into foolish humility before God and the more unworthy it considers itself before God, the more reason dies to its own desire and the more God's Spirit penetrates it and leads it into the highest knowledge, so that it can behold the great miracles of God. For God's Spirit works only in yielded humility. That which does not seek or desire itself, that which within itself desires to be simple before God—this is what the Spirit of God takes hold of and guides into God's miracles. They alone please God who fear and bow before God.

The Yielded Will

For God has not created us for self-sovereignty but rather as a tool of God's miracles, through which God wishes to reveal God's miracles. The yielded will trusts God and hopes for all good from God. But self-will rules itself, for it has broken itself away from God.

Everything that the self-will does is sin and contrary to God. For it is out of the order in which God created it, has gone forth into a disobedient order, and wishes to be its own sovereign.

When one's own will dies to the self, it is free from sin. Then it desires nothing except that which God desires from God's creation. It desires only that for which God created it, that which God wishes to do through it. And although the will is the doing, and must be so, it is nevertheless only a tool of the doing, with which God does what God wishes.

For this is the true faith in a person, that one dies to self, that is, to one's own desire, and that one leads one's desire in all one's intention into God's will, and takes no possessions for oneself, but in all one's doing regards oneself as God's servant and attendant, and thinks that God does all that one does and intends.

In such a will the Spirit of God directs one into real trust and sincerity toward one's neighbor, for one thinks, "I act as I do not for myself but for my God who has called me and directed me into it, as a servant in God's vineyard." One listens always for the voice of one's sovereign, who orders inwardly what one should do.

But the self does what the outward reason from the stars wish. The inner flying devil with his desire directs pleasure into this reason. All that the self does is outside of God's will. It all takes place in the fantasy, so that the wrath of God may accomplish its pleasure with it.

The Will Outside of God's Will

No work outside of God's will can attain to God's realm. It is all a useless carving in the great human laboriousness.[10] For nothing pleases God except what God alone does through the will. There is only one God, in the Being of All Beings. And all that works and labors with God is one spirit with God.

But that which works in its own self in its own will is outside God's dominion and in itself. Indeed, it is in God's almighty dominion with which God directs all life, but not in the holy, divine dominion. Rather, it is in the dominion of nature, with which God governs evil and good. Nothing is called divine that does not proceed and work in God's will.

"All plants," says Christ, "that my Father has not planted must be uprooted and will be burned in the fire" (Matt. 15:13). All human works that are done outside the will of God will be burned in the last fire of God and will be given to the wrath of God, to the abyss of darkness for eternal pleasure. For Christ says, "Who is not with me is against me, and who does not gather with me scatters." That is, who does not work and act in yielded will, in trust in God, only lays waste and scatters. This is not acceptable to God. Nothing pleases God except what God wills with God's Spirit and does through God's tool.

Good and Evil Contend

Therefore whatever takes place by the conclusions of the human self without divine knowledge is all fable and Babel. It is only a work of the stars and of the outer world and is not recognized by God as God's work. Instead it is a mirror of the contending wheel of nature, because good and evil contend with one another. What good builds, evil destroys, and what evil builds, good destroys. And this is the great misery of the futile laboriousness that all belongs in the judgment of God, for the separation of strife.

Therefore who now works and builds in such laboriousness works only for God's judgment. For it is nothing perfect or permanent. It all must go into putrefaction and be separated. For what is worked in God's wrath will be received by it and will be kept in the mystery of its desire until God's Judgment Day, when good and evil are to be separated.

But if one turns around and departs from the self and enters into God's will, then also the good that one worked in the self will be released from the evil that one has worked. For Isaiah spoke, "Though your sins be bloodred, if you turn around and repent, they will become snow-white as wool" (Isa. 1:18). For the evil will be swallowed up in the wrath of God into death, but the good goes forth, like a plant from the wild earth.

BOOK 2

The Yielded Will

Whoever intends to produce something perfect and good, in which one intends to rejoice and enjoy forever, let such a person depart from the self, namely from self-desire, and enter into yieldedness in God's will and work with God.

Although the earthly desire of self adheres to one in flesh and blood, if the soul's will does not take in the desire, the self cannot produce any work. For the yielded will shatters the will's being always and again, so that the wrath of God cannot reach that being. And if it does reach it, which is not totally without possibility and can happen, if the yielded will nevertheless raises high its power, then it stands as a figure before God, a work of triumph in wonder, and can inherit the child-state.[11]

False Desire and Divine Wrath

Therefore it is not good to speak or to act if reason is enkindled in the desire of the self. Otherwise the desire works in God's wrath, by which a person will suffer harm, for one's work will be led into God's wrath and retained there for the great Judgment Day of God.

All false desire—with which a person intends to draw to oneself, through deceit, the world's abundance of one's neighbor, contributing to one's neighbor's ruin—will all be taken into God's wrath and belongs to judgment. Then all will be revealed, all power and being in good and evil will be evident to each person in the mystery of the revelation. All deliberate evil belongs to the judgment of God.

But the one who turns around departs from false desire again, but the work belongs in the fire. Everything should and must be revealed in the end. Therefore God introduced God's effective power into a being, so that God's love and wrath might reveal themselves, and so that in each there might be a play to the honor of God's miracle.

Poison and Pain

And each creature is to know this, that it either remains in that in which God created it, or it runs into opposition and enmity of the will of God and brings itself into torment. For no creature, if it has been created in the darkness, has pain from the darkness, just as a venomous worm has no pain from its own venom. The poison is its life. But if it loses its poison, so that something good enters into it and becomes revealed in its essence, that would be pain and death to it. Likewise evil is pain and death to good.

The person was created in God's love and for paradise, and if one brings oneself into wrath, that is, into poisonous torment and death, then this contrary life is a pain to that person.

If the devil had been created out of the fierce matrix in and for hell and did not have divine essence,[12] then he would have no pain in hell. But because he was created in and for heaven and yet stirred up the quality of darkness in himself and brought himself totally to the dark-world, to him the light is now a pain, that is, an eternal despair of God's grace and a constant enmity. As a result, God cannot endure the devil in God's self and has spat him out. Thus the devil is enraged with his mother that bore him and enraged also with his Father, from whose essence and being he has arisen. This is the eternal nature that holds him prisoner as a traitor out of his place, and amuses itself with him in accordance with the characteristic of wrath and fierceness. Because he refused to help lead God's play of joy, he must now lead God's play of wrath and be an enemy of the good.

Unity and Separation

For God is all: darkness and light, wrath and love, fire and light mercy. But God is called God only in accordance with the light of God's love.

There is an eternal opposition between darkness and light. Neither grasps the other, and neither is the other. Yet there is one single being, though differentiated by the source and by the will, yet it is not a separable being. Only a principle divides it so that each thing is in the other as a nothing. Yet it is there, but not revealed according to the characteristic of that thing in which it is.

For the devil has remained in his dominion, but not in the one in which God created him but rather in the one in which he himself entered—not in the work of the Creation but in the anguished birth of eternity, in the center of nature, in accordance with the characteristic of fierceness for the birthing of darkness and anguish and torment. Indeed the devil is a prince in the place of this world, but in the first principle, in the realm of darkness, in the abyss. Not in the realm of the sun, stars, and elements—there he is neither prince nor sovereign, but only in the part of the fierceness, that is, in the root of the evil of all being. And yet he has not the force with which to act.

The Power of the False Will for Evil

For in all things there is also a good that holds the evil captive and locked up in itself. Thus the devil can only move and rule in the evil when he elevates himself in an evil desire and leads his desire into evil. The lifeless creature cannot do this. But a person can indeed do it through the lifeless creature if one brings the center of one's will, with the desire, out of the eternal center into the creature. This is incantation and false magic. The soul's desire is of eternal origin, but when a person leads it into evil by means of a false will, there the devil's will can also enter in.

The Devil's Power in Chaos

For the primordial state of souls and angels is, from eternity, one. But from the time of this world, the devil has nothing,[13] except in the great chaos. Where the chaos enkindles itself in the eternal fierceness, there the devil is busy, as in war and conflict, also in great thunderstorms without water. In the fire he goes only as far as the chaos goes. He cannot go farther. He also goes in the downpour, that is, in the chaos, but he cannot direct it, for he is not master in it but rather servant.

Thus the creature with desire awakens good and evil, life and death. The human and angelic desire stands in the center of the eternal nature that has no beginning. There desire enkindles itself in evil or in good, whose work it accomplishes.

The Will Gone Astray

Now God moreover created each thing in and for that in which it should be: the angels in and for heaven, and the human being in and for paradise. If then the desire of the creature departs from its own mother, it enters into opposition and enmity, and in this it is tormented with the opposition, and a false will arises in a good one. From this the good will enters again into its nothing, that is, into the end of nature and creature, and abandons the creature in its own evil, as is seen in Lucifer and also in Adam. If God's love-will had not come to meet him and from grace entered once more into humankind, there could be no good will in the human being.

Therefore all speculation and enquiry into God's will is a futile thing without a turning around of the soul's mind. When the soul's mind is captive in its own desire of the earthly life, it cannot grasp God's will. It only runs in the self, from one path to another, and yet finds no rest. For self-desire always leads to disquiet.

Sinking into Divine Mercy

But when the soul's mind sinks completely into God's mercy and desires to die to its self and desires God's will as guide and understanding—so that it might understand and regard itself as a nothing that wills nothing apart from what God wills—then if the desire of wrath in the earthly flesh, along with the devil's imagination, approaches and assaults the soul's will, then the yielded desire cries out to God, "Abba, dear Father, deliver me from evil."[14] The yielded will then works only in itself,[15] as St. Paul says, "If I sin, I do not do it but rather the sin that dwells in the flesh" (Rom. 7:20). Again: "So I now serve the law of God with my mind but the law of sin with the flesh" (Rom. 7:25).

The Contest between the Yielded Will and the Will of the Flesh

Paul does not mean that the soul's mind is to acquiesce to the flesh's will, but rather that sin is so strong in the flesh, that is, in the awakened wrath of God in the self, that one is often led into delight through force, through a false echo of godless people, or through a glimpse of worldly haughtiness, so that one is completely drowned out with regard to the yielded will and is presently ruled by force.

And so when sin is effected in the flesh, the wrath wishes to amuse itself with it and grasps at the yielded will. So the yielded will cries out to God for deliverance from evil, so that God might wish to remove the sin away from the will and lead sin into the center, namely into death, so that it might die.

And St. Paul says further, "So there is now nothing condemnable to those who are in Christ Jesus" (Rom. 8:1). Those who are called according to the purpose,[16] that is, the purpose of God into which God called humankind, are called again into that same calling so that they stand once more in the purpose of God, in which God created humankind in God's likeness and image. As long as one's own will stands in the self, it is not in the purpose and calling of God; it is not called, for it has departed from its place.

Becoming a Child of God

But when the soul's mind turns around once more to its calling, that is, into yieldedness, the will is in the calling of God, that is, in the place and for the purpose for which God created it. Then it has the might to become a child of God; as it is written, Christ has given us the might to become God's children.[17] The might that Christ has given us is God's purpose, in which God created humankind in God's image. God in Christ has again brought this might into humanity, and has given might to that might to crush the head of sin in the flesh, that is, the will and desire of the serpent. That is, the yielded will in Christ treads upon the head of the desire of the sinful serpent-will, and kills again sins that had been committed. The might given becomes a death to death, and a might of life to life.

Therefore no one has an excuse, as if one could not will. Indeed, while one remains stuck in the self, in one's own desire, and serves only the law of sin in the flesh, one cannot. For one is constrained and is the servant of sin. But when the center of the soul's mind turns around and turns into God's obedience and will, then one can.

Now the center of the soul's mind is from eternity, from God's omnipotence; it can bring itself where it wishes. For what is from the eternal has no law, but the will has a law: to obey God. And the will is born out of the soul's mind and must not displace itself from that in which God created it.

Thus God nevertheless created the will of the soul's mind in and for paradise, to be a playmate in the divine realm of joy, from which it must not displace itself. But now since it has displaced itself, God has again led God's will into flesh and has given us might in this newly led will, to lead our will into it and to enkindle a new light in it, to become God's children once again.

God Wills No Evil

God hardens no one, but one's own will, which persists in the flesh of sin, hardens the soul's mind. For the will leads the vanity of this world into the soul's mind, so that the soul's mind remains locked up.

God, insofar as God is and is called God, can will no evil. For there is only one unified will in God, and it is eternal love, a desire for likeness, namely, power, beauty, and virtue.

God desires only what is like God's desire. God's desire accepts nothing except what the desire itself is.

God accepts no sinner into God's power unless the sinner departs from sin and enters into God with the desire. And those who come to God, God will not cast out.[18] In Christ, God has given to the will an open gate and says, "Come to me all of you who are burdened with sin. I will refresh you. Take my yoke upon you," that is, the cross of enmity in the flesh, which was the yoke of Christ, who had to bear it for the sins of all people. The yielded will must also take this upon itself in the evil, earthly flesh of sin, and carry it after Christ in patience, in the hope of salvation. And with the yielded will of the soul, it must evermore, in Christ's will and Spirit, crush the serpent's head in God's wrath, and kill and break the earthly will. The yielded will is not to allow itself to rest or to lie in a soft bed when sin is committed and think, "I will do penance for this at some point."

To Overpower the Earthly Will, Sink into Christ's Death

No, no, in this soft bed the earthly will only grows strong, fat, and lascivious. But as soon as the breath of God stirs itself in you, and points out your sin, then the soul's will should sink itself into the suffering and death of Christ, and firmly wrap itself in it and take the suffering of Christ into itself as a possession, and should be sovereign over the death of sin,[19] and shatter and kill the earthly will in Christ's death.

The earthly will must die, even though it does not wish to. Therefore make enmity against the lustful, earthly flesh. Do not give it what it wishes to have. Let it fast and hunger until the arousal ceases. Regard the will of the flesh as your foe, and do not do what the desire in the flesh wishes. Thus you will bring a death to the death in the flesh. Pay no attention to the scorn of the world. Think that they scorn only your foe, and that your foe has become the world's fool. For yourself, consider your foe as your fool, whom Adam awakened in you and has declared your false heir. Cast out of the house the female servant's son, the foreign son that God did not give to you in Adam at the beginning to be in the house of life.[20] For the female servant must not inherit with the free (Gal. 4:30).

A New Mind of the Soul

The earthly will is only the son of the female servant. For the four elements should have been the servant to humankind, but Adam led them into the child-state. Therefore God said to Abraham when revealing to him the covenant of promise, "Cast out the female servant's son, for he must not inherit with the free woman."[21] The free woman is Christ,[22] whom God, out of grace, brought into the flesh for us, that is, a new mind, where the will—understand the eternal will of the soul—can draw and drink the water of eternal life. Of this Christ says, "Whoever will drink of this water that Christ will give to us, for that person it will swell up into a fountain of eternal life" (John 4:13). The fountain-source is a renewal of the soul's mind, that is, the eternal constellation of the eternal nature, that is, the characteristic of the spiritual creature.

Therefore I say, all speculation about God, whatever name it may have, by which a person may imagine a path to God, is a futile, useless thing without the new mind of the soul.

There is no other path to God than a new mind of the soul that turns from evil and enters into repentance for its committed sins, departs from iniquity and no more wills it, but rather entwines its will in Christ's death and with earnestness dies to the sins of the soul in Christ's death, so that the soul's mind no longer wills sin. Even though all devils were behind it and entered into the flesh with their desire, the soul's will must stand still in the death of Christ, hide itself there, and wish nothing except God's mercy.

No hypocrisy or outward consolation helps at all, where one wishes to cover up the scoundrel of sin in the flesh with Christ's payment while remaining standing in the self. Christ said, "Unless you turn around and become as children, you will not see the realm of God" (Matt. 18:3). Indeed, the new mind of the soul must become as a child that knows nothing of sin. Christ further said, "You must be born anew, otherwise you will not see God's realm" (John 3:3). A totally new will must arise from Christ's death. Indeed, it must be born out of Christ's entrance into humanity and rise in Christ's resurrection.

Die in Christ's Death

If this is to happen, the soul's will must first die in Christ's death, for in Adam it received the son of the female servant, that is, sin. One must first cast sin out from the will, and the poor captive soul must entwine itself in the death of Christ—with earnestness, with all that the soul is—so that the son of the female servant, namely the sin in it, might die in Christ's death. Indeed, sin must die in the soul's will; otherwise there can be no vision of God. For the earthly will in sin and in God's wrath will not see God, but rather Christ who came into the flesh will see God. The soul must put on Christ's Spirit and flesh. In this earthly hut it cannot inherit God's realm,[23] although the realm of sin outwardly is attached to the soul. This hut must decay in the earth and rise in new power.

There is neither hypocrisy nor mere verbal forgiveness. We must not be outwardly accepted children, but rather children inwardly born from God into a new person who is yielded to God.

All hypocrisy, such that we say, "Christ has paid and made satisfaction for sin. He has died for our sin," is all false and a deception if we do not also die to sin in him,[24] put on his merit in a new obedience, and live in it.

The person who has Christ's sufferings as consolation is the one who becomes inimical and angry toward sin. One who does not willingly see, hear, or taste sin, who is hostile to sin, who wishes eagerly to do at all times what is right and good, if one only knew what one should do—such a person has put on Christ's Spirit and will. Outward hypocrisy of the outwardly accepted child-state is false and futile.

The Child-State

The work that occurs only in the outward flesh does not effect the child-state, but the work of Christ in the Spirit, which is efficacious with the outward work and manifests itself as a new light and reveals the child-state in the outward work of the flesh—this both is and produces the child-state.

For if the eye of the soul is light, then the entire body is light in all its members.[25] If anyone boasts of the child-state and allows the body to burn in sin, or lies in the bonds of the devil, one is not yet capable of the child-state. And if one does not find the earnest will for good deeds in love burning within, then one's pretense is only a speculation of reason from the self, which cannot see God unless the self is born anew and shows itself in the power of the child-state. For no fire is without light. If God's fire is in the soul's mind, it will indeed shine forth and do what God wishes to have it do.

But you say, "I have a will to do so. I would eagerly do it, but I am constrained. I cannot."

Indeed, dear soiled block of wood,[26] that is so. God draws you to the child-state, but you do not wish it. Your soft pillow in evil is much more beloved to you. You set the joy of earthly evil above God's joy. You are stuck entirely in the self and live in accordance with the law of sin that detains you. You cannot die to the sensual pleasure of the flesh. Therefore you are not in the child-state. God nevertheless draws you to it, but you yourself do not wish it. Ah, how fine Adam would have thought it to be, if one received him into heaven with this will and set the evil child, full of falsehood, on God's throne. Lucifer also wished it so, but he was spat out.

The death of the evil will causes pain. No one wishes for it. We would all gladly be children, if one would accept us with this pelt, but it can in no way be so. This world perishes; therefore the outward life must also die. What possible good can the child-state be to me in a mortal body?

Whoever wants to inherit the child-state must also put on a new person that can inherit the child-state and is like the deity. God wishes to have no sinner in heaven, but rather only newborn children who have put on heaven.

Therefore it is not an easy thing to become or be children of God, as one represents it to us. It is indeed easy to one who has put on the child-state, whose light shines and whose joy is therein. But to turn the soul's mind and shatter the self, there must be a rigorous, unrelenting earnestness, and such purpose that, though body and soul were to snap apart, the will would yet remain steadfast and not again enter into the self.

Christ Born Within

This must be wrestled with until the dark, tough, locked-up center bursts and the spark in the center inflames. From there immediately the noble lily-branch sprouts forth, as from a divine mustard-seed, as Christ says.[27] There must be earnest prayer with great humility, and for a while one must be a fool to one's own reason and see oneself as foolish, until Christ takes a form in this new incarnation.[28]

And then, when Christ is born, immediately Herod comes and wishes to kill the little child,[29] and hunts for the child outwardly by persecution and inwardly by temptation to determine whether this lily branch will be strong enough to shatter the devil's realm that is revealed in the flesh.

This serpent-treader is led into the wilderness, after he [Christ born within] is first baptized with the Holy Spirit. One is tempted as to whether one wishes to remain in yieldedness in God's will. One must therefore stand steadfast so that, if necessary, one would forsake all that is earthly—indeed, even the outward life—for the sake of the child-state.

Nonpossessiveness

No temporal honor or good must be given preference to the child-state. Rather one must with one's will forsake all this and not regard it as one's own and consider oneself only as its servant, who with it serves one's sovereign in obedience. One must forsake all possessions of this world—not that one does not or must not possess it. Only one's heart must forsake it and not bring one's will into it and regard it as one's own. Otherwise one has not power to serve the needy with it.

The Character of Yieldedness

The self serves only the temporal being, but yieldedness rules over all that is under it. The self must do what the devil in the sensual pleasure of the flesh and the arrogant life would have.[30] But yielded-ness treads on this with the feet of the soul's mind. The self disdains what is simple, but yieldedness lies down in the dust with the simple and says, "I wish to be simple and understand nothing, so that my reason will not raise itself up and sin. I wish to lie in the forecourts of my God, at God's feet, so that I may serve my sovereign in what-ever God will have of me. I wish to know nothing, so that the com-mands of my sovereign may lead and guide me, so that I do only what God wishes and does through me. I want to sleep in myself until the Lord awakens me with God's Spirit. And if God does not wish to do so, then I want to rest eternally in God in stillness and to await God's command."

The Need for True Faith

Dear brothers and sisters, one boasts now in faith, but where is faith? The current faith is a history. Where is the child who believes that Jesus is born? If there were such a child who believed that Jesus was born, that child would surely draw near to the little child Jesus, to receive and care for the little child Jesus. Ah, but it is only a his-torical faith, and a mere academic knowledge, and much more an arousal of the conscience: that the Jews killed him,[31] that he went away from this world, that he is not king on earth of the beastly people, that a person can do as one wishes, that a person need not die to sin and the evil pleasures. The self, the evil child, rejoices that it can live in fatness and fatten the devil.

This proves that the true faith has never, since Christ's time, been sicker and weaker than now. The world nevertheless loudly cries out, "We have the true faith." And they quarrel over a child. This has never been worse since people have been on earth.

Show Forth the Child Jesus

If you are Zion, the newborn and found-again child, then demon-strate your power and virtue and show forth the little child Jesus, from you, so that one can see that you are his nurse. If not, then the children of Christ will say that you have found only the child of history, that is, the cradle of the child.

Where do you have the little child Jesus, you apostate with the history and false appearance of faith? How will the little child Jesus visit you in the Father's characteristic, in your own chaos that you have fattened? The child calls to you in love, but you do not wish to hear, for your eyes are locked up in covetousness and sensual pleasure. Therefore one day the sound of the trumpet with a fierce thunderclap will blast your chaos, and awaken you to determine whether you wish once gain to seek and find the little child Jesus.

Dear brothers and sisters, it is a time of seeking, finding, and earnestness. Whom it concerns, it concerns. One who watches will hear and see it. But one who sleeps in sin and in the fat days of one's belly says, "All is peace and quiet. We hear no sound from the Lord." But the Lord's voice has sounded to the end of the earth, and a smoke ascends, and in the midst of the smoke there is a great brilliance of a splendor. Amen. Hallelujah. Amen.

Rejoice in the Lord in Zion, for all mountains and hills are full of God's sovereignty. God shoots up like a plant[32]—who will restrain it? Hallelujah.

THE INCARNATION
OF JESUS CHRIST

V ON DER MENSCHWERDUNG JESU CHRISTI, or *De
incarnatione Verbi*, according to the Latinized title Boehme gave
to the work, presents spiritual rebirth through Jesus Christ by means
of faith as the fulfillment of God's image, which was created in the
first Adam and restored in the conception of Jesus in the Virgin
Mary. Spiritual rebirth is the work of Jesus Christ through his suffering, death, and resurrection, restoring the image of God to believers and completing God's original intentions in the creation of Adam
and in the incarnation of the second Adam, Jesus Christ, in the Virgin Mary. The German title of the book means *The Incarnation* [lit-
erally, "becoming human"] *of Jesus Christ.*[1] While the book rehearses
the virginal conception of Jesus Christ as a human being who is simultaneously full of divine essence, the point of the book is neither
a rehearsal of the biblical accounts of the conception of Jesus, nor a
chronological telling of his life, suffering, death, and resurrection.
For Boehme, that would be merely historical faith, inadequate for
the challenges of his time and insufficient to effect spiritual rebirth.
The true incarnation of Jesus Christ is also contemporaneous with

each believer, who by means of faith dies to sin, is transformed into a virginal person by the virginal Jesus Christ, and moves out of the wrath of being a condemned sinner into the mercy of forgiveness and spiritual resurrection.

The Latinized title of the book is not exactly the same as the German, despite a sense in the seventeenth century that the concepts of the two different languages referred to the same event. *De incarnatione Verbi* means "the incarnation of the word," which Boehme fills out in the book as "the incarnation of the word of God." This title points to the word's eternal existence with God, and the power of God's word to transform sinners through God's mercy and love, creating a new birth and spiritually new people. The "word" to which Boehme refers is not merely the written words of the Bible, the Gospels, or the biblical texts about Jesus's conception and birth. Again, such a word would be merely historical and not sufficiently powerful to give spiritual rebirth. The "word" of Boehme's title is related to his oft-repeated phrase, *Verbo Fiat,* which we have translated as the "creative utterance." It points to God's speech as having the power to generate life, both in creation and in spiritual rebirth (which is like a re-creation for Boehme).

Boehme wrote *The Incarnation of Jesus Christ* in 1620, a very productive year for his writing. He saw this piece as a companion to his earlier, immense tome, *The Three Principles of Divine Being. The Incarnation of Jesus Christ* is a shorter and more focused work that takes as its main theme spiritual rebirth.

The book consists of three main parts. Part 1 contains fourteen chapters. It reviews the creation of Adam out of divine essence, androgynous and espoused to Sophia, the female aspect of God personified as Wisdom (Sophia). Boehme describes how the conception of Jesus Christ in the Virgin Mary reversed the loss of God's image in humanity, which occurred when the first Adam fell into sin. The final chapter of part 1 stresses the importance of spiritual rebirth. The ten chapters of part 2 recount how spiritual rebirth occurs as believers participate spiritually in the suffering, death, and resurrection of Jesus Christ. The final chapter of part 2 emphasizes how the image of God inhabits (takes on) humanity in all who are spiritually reborn. Part 3, consisting of eight chapters, focuses on faith as the power by which new birth comes to people. The final chapter highlights how one becomes a child of God through rebirth.

In each of the three parts of the book, Boehme links the incarnation of Jesus Christ as a concrete person in history to Christ's spiritual incarnation in each believer. Each of the three parts of the book traces a different path in guiding seekers to rebirth and their encounter with Christ.

Part 1 of *The Incarnation of Jesus Christ* reviews how the image of God was imparted to Adam at the Creation. Adam was fully in God's image because he was created from divine essence and was made androgynous. Because Adam desired his own will rather than God's will, Adam lost his virginal image and fell into sin and into material life. God restored the divine image to humankind in the virginal conception of Jesus Christ in the Virgin Mary. Because he bore the full image of God, Christ's incarnation reversed Adam's fall into sin. Near the end of part 1, Boehme reworks the theme of restoring the image of God by using his alchemical language. He compares the spiritual rebirth to the alchemical process of extracting gold from coarse stone with the help of a transforming agent (a tincture). For the spiritual rebirth, that agent is virginity from heaven. In his incarnation, Jesus embodied that virginity, even as he was born of a virgin, namely Mary.

In part 2, Boehme focuses on the incarnation of Jesus Christ in humans through the new birth, focusing not on the conception of Christ, but on Christ's suffering, death, and resurrection. Although Boehme employs the language of his cosmology in these chapters, ultimately he links rebirth to a spiritual participation in Christ's death and resurrection in order for people to become children of God.

By describing faith as the "tree of Christian faith" in part 3 of *The Incarnation of Jesus Christ*, Boehme portrays the incarnation of Christ as the union of Jesus Christ with believers contemporaneously. Faith is the tree trunk to which branches are joined in order to live. By such faith, believers are united to Jesus Christ, so that rebirth makes their wills desire God's will. Human will cannot trust human works, but should only seek God's will. In this way the forgiveness of sins is not a matter of learning historical propositions about Jesus. Faith lives when the new birth awakens it and allows Jesus Christ to dwell in people, restoring the image of God that was with Christ all along. What was intended for Adam in the beginning of the Creation is possible for all who will believe and receive rebirth. In the conclusion, Boehme admonishes that this new birth is not available to hypocritical preachers and theologians who trust in propositions rather than receive rebirth in Christ.

The passage from *The Incarnation of Jesus Christ* translated in this book brings out very clearly the interplay between Christ's historical incarnation and the spiritual incarnation that occurs through the spiritual rebirth of believers. It clearly illustrates the parallel meanings that Boehme deploys to explain the mystery of incarnation, not just in the virginal conception of Jesus, but in the transformative spiritual encounter believers have with Jesus in the present. In this interplay of parallel meanings, the incarnation of Jesus Christ has enduring efficacy.

THE INCARNATION
OF JESUS CHRIST

CHAPTER 9

For us poor children of Eve, it is highly necessary to know this, for our eternal salvation lies therein. For it is the gate of Emmanuel, and the whole Christian faith stands in it. It is the gate of the greatest mystery, for here lies concealed the secret of humankind in which one is the image and likeness of God.

The Core of Religious Doctrine: Creation, Fall, Rebirth

For our whole religion consists of three parts that we promote and teach. First, concerning creation: what essence, being, and characteristic a person is; whether one is eternal or not eternal, and how that is possible; what really is the primordial human condition; from where has the person originated?

And then the second: because so much is said and taught about the Fall, we must see what the Fall really was, since we are mortal on account of the Fall and subject to evil and the source of fierceness.

And third: because God wishes to receive us again into grace, for the sake of which God also has given laws and teachings, and validated them with great miraculous deeds, what really is the new birth? Because we see that we must die, in what power and spirit can we become newly born and rise from death?

Eternal and Earthly Virginity

All this we find prefigured in two images, namely in the eternal, holy virginity and also in the earthly, fragile virginity. And we find the new birth quite plainly and clearly in the figure of Christ. For Adam was the person created in the eternal virginity, that is, God's being, where the image and likeness of God is seen as in a mirror and known by the Spirit of God. Adam had the virginity as a possession, as the true transforming agent of love in the light. This transforming agent is desirous of the fire as the characteristic of the essences, so that it might be a burning life in power and glory, and may be a birthing woman in the fire's essence, which is not possible in the light's essence without the fire.

The Virginity in God's Wisdom

And we recognize therefore a virginity in God's Wisdom, in the desiring will of the divine being from eternity: not a woman who gives birth, rather a figure in the mirror of the Wisdom of God, a pure, chaste image without being, and yet in the essence; but not revealed in the fire's essence, rather in the light's source.

The Earthly Corrupted the Heavenly

God created this image into a being out of all three principles, so that it might be a likeness in accordance with the Godhead and eternity, as a complete mirror of the ground and of the unfathomable (or unground), and a mirror of the Spirit and also of being. And it was created out of the eternal, not for fragility. But because the earthly and fragile depend on the eternal, the earthly desire has introduced itself into the eternal heavenly desire and has infected the heavenly characteristic. For it wished to dwell in the eternal but was corrupted in the fierceness of God.

Thus the earthly quality corrupted the heavenly, and became the chaos of the heavenly quality, as is to be recognized in earth and stones. These indeed have their origin from the eternal, but are corrupted in the fierceness and in the fire's quality. And the creative command has made earth and stone out of the eternal being, for the sake of which a day of separation is appointed, when each thing is to return to its ether and to be tried by fire.[2]

So also Adam was created in the virginity in God's Wisdom, but was seized by the fierceness and wrath of God and therefore also immediately became corrupted and earthly. And as the earth perishes and must be tried by fire and return again into that which it once was, so also the person, who is to enter again into the virginity in which they were created. But it was not possible for the person to rise from the fierce death and enter into a new birth, because the person's virginity was closed up in death. Therefore God made for the human a woman out of him. Therefore the Godhead had to move itself, and to reveal and to make alive again that which had been closed up.

The Heart of God Moved Itself

This happened in Mary, the enclosed virgin. Understand this: in the virginity that Adam inherited from God's wisdom, not from the earthly part of the third principle, rather of the heavenly, holy part of the second principle. This principle had been closed up in the earthly death, in the anger of God, by means of the earthly imagination and intuition. This principle was as if dead, as the earth also appeared as dead. Therefore the heart of God has moved itself, has shattered death on the cross, and has born life once more.

And for us the birth and incarnation of Christ is a powerful being, in that the entire unfathomable heart of God has moved itself. Thus the heavenly being, which had been closed up in death, has once more become alive. As a result we can now say with good reason that God has resisted God's own wrath, insofar as God has opened God's self again, by means of the center of God's heart that has filled eternity without foundation or limit. God has deprived death of its force and shattered its sting of fierceness and wrath, since love and gentleness have revealed themselves in the wrath; they have extinguished the force of the fire.

We Become Pregnant

And even more so it is a great joy to us people, because God has revealed God's self in our dead and deceased virginity, and therefore through everything. The word or the power of the life of God has entered again into humankind, that is, into the dead and, so to speak, forsaken virginity, and has revealed again the virginal life. Consequently we rejoice and enter with our imagination into the center, where God has revealed God's self in humankind, that is, in the incarnation of God's Son. Therefore we become pregnant with God's revealed word and the power of the heavenly, divine being, indeed nothing foreign, but yet foreign with respect to the earthliness. We become pregnant in our imagination, which we lead into the incarnation of God's Son. The word has revealed itself everywhere also in each person's life-light, and the only thing missing is that the soul's spirit give itself into it, so that the soul's spirit put on the eternal virginity again, not as a garment but as its own essence in which God is born. For Mary was born earthly like all the daughters of Eve, but the covenant of the love of God indicated in her essence that God wanted to open life in her again.

Mary's Earthly Virginity

And we can in no way say regarding Mary's virginity according to the earthly life before the blessing,[3] before God's heart moved itself, that she had been a completely perfect virgin, like the first virgin before the Fall; rather she was a natural daughter of Eve. But we do say with good reason that in Mary, as well as in all of Adam's children, the eternal virginity in the covenant of the promise lay enclosed, just like in death, and yet in God had not decayed. For the name Jesus, from God's center or heart, from eternity placed its image in the virgin of the Wisdom of God as with a mirror. The name Jesus is opposed to the Father's center, that is, the center of the fire and fierceness, not in the fierceness of fire, in the fire's essence, but in the love in light, in the light essence. And the human was provided with the same essence in the name Jesus, before the foundation of the world was laid, when Adam was still in the heavenly essence without a natural or creaturely being. For the Fall was known in the wisdom before the human became a creature, and this was so according to the fire's characteristic, not in the light's characteristic, rather according to the first principle.

Therefore we now say in accordance with our deep knowledge of Mary that before the time of the revelation and the message of the angel, she was a virgin like Eve, when Eve went out of paradise. She was then indeed a virgin. But the real virginity was hidden in her and infected with earthly longing.[4] And the animal characteristic was revealed in her, for the earthly imagination shattered the heavenly characteristic so that she was a woman and not a chaste virgin without blemish. For only one part of her partook of the heavenly virginity; the other part was Adam. And so, no pure, true virgin has been born from Eve who could be completely virginal. Chaos destroyed the virginity in all, until the hero of the battle came, who was a completely manly virgin in God's wisdom according to the heavenly wisdom. And the earthly hung on him, but the heavenly ruled over the earthly. For Adam should also have been thus, but he did not prevail.

The Goal of the Covenant

Therefore we say with good reason that Mary was Joachim's daughter, born of Anna, and her being was essentially in herself, in accordance with the earthly part. And then we say that she was the daughter of God's covenant, that God had stuck in her the goal of the new birth, that the whole Old Testament had looked toward the same goal and that all prophets prophesied the same goal.[5] The same goal has been blessed, for God had given God's own self into this goal with God's own mercy, with the covenant of the promise. And the word stood in the promise in the covenant and in the life's light against the wrath. The first world before and after the Flood was saved in the same covenant that God set before God's self as a virginal mirror. For the eternal virginity appeared in the covenant, as in God's mirror, and therein the Godhead delighted itself. For when Israel kept the covenant and did the work of the covenant, that was accepted by God as if humankind were in the mirror of God's wisdom. And even if Israel was earthly and evil, nevertheless God dwelt in Israel in God's covenant in the wisdom according to God's love and mercy.

Thus the works of the law were before God in the mirror,[6] until the life was born again out of the covenant, until the fulfillment came. The works in the mirror then ceased, and the works of the fulfillment commenced once again in flesh and blood in the heavenly being. For the beginning was in Mary. When the angel brought her the message, and she said, "May it happen to me as you have said" (Luke 1:38), at once the center of life in the word of God, that is, the heart of God, moved itself in her dead, heavenly seed and made it alive once more, and the impregnation began. For all three principles of the Godhead were moved, and the Godhead held captive the divine transforming substance in the dead heavenly being. Not that God stood without being; rather, humankind was dead to the heavenly seed. And now the heart of God came into death with living, divine being, and awoke the dead being. It did not at this time take away the earthly quality; rather, it entered into the earthly quality.[7] For the true life was to be led in through death and God's wrath, which happened on the cross, when death was shattered and the fierceness taken captive and extinguished and conquered by love.

A Heavenly Virgin by Conceiving Jesus

Therefore we now understand what Mary became by the conception, namely a true, pure virgin in accordance with the heavenly part. For when the heart of God moved itself and day dawned in her, then the light of the radiance and purity of God shone in her. For her dead virginity, that is, God's Wisdom, became revealed and alive, for she was filled with the divine virginity, that is, God's Wisdom. And in this same Wisdom and divine being, as well as in the dead and now alive being, the word became flesh in sulfur, by the center of nature, out of the Father's essence and out of Mary's essence. Out of death came a life, a fruit with both transforming agents perfect, because both were now one. And because Adam had become a man, Christ also became a man according to the external world. For Eve's image in the woman's infused essence was not to remain. Rather, Adam's image was to remain, when he was a man and also a woman. But one of the signs had to appear, according to the might of the external creative command. And so that the hero in combat once again would be established in all three principles, the hero in combat received the male sign. For the man has the fire's transforming substance, that is, the Father's characteristic. Therefore the Father is the strength and might of all things, and the Son is his love. Thus the word became human in the female essence, but became a man, so that his love might extinguish the wrath and fierceness in the Father. For the transforming substance of Venus has the water-quality, and the woman has the transforming substance of Venus. So the fire was to be extinguished by the water of eternal life,[8] and the Father's burning essence in the fire was to be once more extinguished.

But we now know Mary, the mother of Christ according to flesh, soul, and spirit, as a pure, chaste virgin in the blessing. For this is her blessing: that God revealed God's self in her. She carried the word of life in her body,[9] and the word moved itself within her. Not that Mary moved the word; rather, the word moved Mary, both the fruit that she bore and also her soul, as well as the portion of the dead being, so that her soul was at once encircled with divine, living being. This did not happen according to the earthly part, namely according to the third principle, but rather according to the heavenly part, namely according to the second principle, so that what is earthly merely hung upon her. For along with the word of life, her soul was to enter through death and the wrath of the Father into the heavenly divine quality. Therefore her external person had to die to the earthly quality, so that the external person could live to God. And so, because she was blessed and carried the goal of the covenant, her body did not decay. For what is heavenly has swallowed what is earthly and holds captive what is eternal—a miracle to the honor of God. In eternity it is not to be forgotten that in her, God became human.[10]

Mary Lives through the Blessing

But some say that she remained fully in death and was fully decayed. These should truly reconsider their judgment, for what has been highly blessed is imperishable. Her heavenly part of the divine being, which has blessed her, is imperishable. Otherwise it would have to follow that God's being, which was in the blessing, would once more have fallen and died, as happened in Adam. For the sake of that death, however, God became human, so that God could restore life. Mary has indeed died according to the external life, that is, the earthly quality. But she lives according to the blessing in God's being and also in her own being; not in the four elements but rather in the root of the four elements, that is, in one element that holds the other four closed up in itself, in paradise and the pure element, in the divine being, in the life of God.

What the Word Accomplished

We say therefore that Mary is greater than any other daughter of Adam, in that God has placed the goal of God's covenant in her. And she alone of all Eve's daughters attained the blessing, that is, the pure, virginal chastity that was destroyed in all the daughters of Eve. But with regard to her, the virginity stood in the covenant, until the word of life highly blessed her. Thus she became a true, pure, chaste virgin in whom God was born. For Christ also said to the Jews, "I am from above, but you are from below. I am not of this world, but you are of this world" (John 8:23).[11] If he had become human in an earthly vessel and not in a pure, heavenly, chaste virgin, then he would indeed have been of this world. But he thus became human in the heavenly virgin, and the earthly quality merely hung on him. For the essence of the soul was infected in us poor children of humankind, and he was to lead our soul in the heavenly essence in himself through the fire of God into the Holy Threeness.[12] For this applies to the soul, because the soul had been taken out of the eternal, but God did not wish to forsake the soul.

Therefore when asked, what kind of material it was into which God's word and heart had given itself and made a body for itself, whether it was foreign material that came from heaven, or whether it was Mary's essence and seed, this is our answer. God's heart was never without being, for God's dwelling place is from eternity in the light. And the power in the light is the heart or word that God has spoken from eternity. And the speaking was the Holy Spirit of God, who goes forth out of the power of the light, out of the spoken word, and into what is spoken forth. And what is spoken forth is God's wonder and wisdom. This has in itself the divine mirror of wisdom, in which the Spirit of God sees and reveals wonders.

Therefore understand that the word out of the heart of God the Father has revealed itself at once in Mary's essence and being,[13] that is, in her own seed—understand, in human seed. The word has taken into itself Mary's seed that was dead and blind with regard to God, and awakened it to life. The living being came into the half-killed and took the half-killed for a body,[14] not as a perishable body that was to cease, but rather as an eternal body that was to remain eternally, for the eternal life was born once again.

Christ's Creatureliness

Thus the being of eternity in God, in God's entire unfathomable depth, and the being of the dead Adam in humanity, become one wholly unified being, so that the creature Christ with his being filled at once the whole Father who is without limit or foundation. But the creaturely soul remained and is a creature. And in accordance with the third principle, that is, pertaining to the creature, this Christ is a creature and a king of humankind. And in accordance with the second principle, Christ is also a child of the unfathomable Father. What the Father in his unfathomable depth is, that the Son is in his creature. For the power in the creature is one power with the power outside the creature, one being in which angels and humans dwell. The power bestows paradise and joyful bliss, but to humanity it also bestows flesh and blood. Therefore the creature is and remains one creature; uncreated, yet born, one part out of God from eternity and the other part out of humanity. And God and humankind have become one person, one Christ, one God, one Lord, one Holy Trinity in humanity and also simultaneously everywhere. Thus when we see Christ, we see the Holy Trinity in one image. Christ's creatureliness is like our human image. He is our high priest and king, our brother, our Emmanuel. His power is our power, if we are reborn from God in him through faith. He is not foreign or frightening to us, but rather is our transforming substance of love. Through his power he is the revitalizing of our soul, of our life, and of our soul's bliss. When we find him, we find our helper, just as Adam should have found him, but he let himself be deceived and in the end found a woman. So he said, "This is flesh of my flesh and bone of my bone," and he took her to himself to be his companion (Gen. 2:23).

Virginity Lost and Found

So when our soul finds Christ, it says, "This is my virginal husband that I had lost in Adam, at the time an earthly woman was made from him. Now I have once again found my beloved virginal husband from my body. Now I never again want Christ to leave me. Christ is mine, my flesh and blood, my strength and power that I lost in Adam. I want to keep Christ." Oh, what a friendly keeping! A friendly imparting of qualities, beauty, fruit, power, and virtue.

Thus the poor soul finds the transforming agent of its lost light and its beloved virgin. And in the woman the noble bridegroom is found. The matrix of Venus had always lusted after this bridegroom but had found only an earthly male sulfur, and had to allow itself to become pregnant with earthly seed. Here the soul receives the transforming agent of the true fire and man, so that it also becomes a true male virgin as Adam was in his innocence.

CHAPTER 10

Worldly Reason Cannot Grasp the Incarnation

People have disputed much about the incarnation of Jesus Christ, but almost blindly, and out of this they have produced many opinions. With these opinions, they spin people around, but they leave behind the true incarnation in which our salvation lies. The cause of all this was that people sought salvation in external farce and trickery and not in the true goal. If one had entered into the incarnation of Christ and was born of God, no disputing would have been necessary. The Spirit of God reveals the incarnation of Christ to each person in one's own self, and without the Spirit there is no finding it. For how will we find in the reason of this world that which is not of this world? And external reason, we hardly find a glimmer of it, but in God's Spirit is the true finding.

The incarnation of Christ is such a mystery that the external reason knows nothing of it, for it happened in all three principles. And it cannot be fathomed, unless one knows thoroughly the first person in his creation, before the Fall. For Adam ought to have given birth out of himself to the second person, with the character of the Holy Trinity, in which the name Jesus was embodied. But this could not be. Therefore a second Adam had to come, to whom this was possible, for Christ is the virgin image with the character of the Holy Trinity. Christ was conceived in God's love and born in this world. Adam had divine being, and his soul was from the first principle, from the Father's characteristic. His soul was to direct itself by means of the imagination into the Father's heart, that is, into the word and spirit of love and purity, and to eat of the being of love. Then the soul would have preserved in itself God's being in the word of life, and would have become pregnant by the power from the heart of God. For thereby his soul from itself would have imagined itself into its being, and with itself have impregnated its being. Thus a complete likeness in accordance with the first image would have arisen through imagination and through the submission of the soul's will, and would have conceived in the power of being.

Christ Succeeded Where Adam Failed

But because this could not be in Adam, on account of the earthliness that adhered to him, it happened in the second Adam, Christ. Christ was conceived in such a manner through God's imagination and entrance into the image of the first Adam.

And so we are to recognize that, while the first Adam set his imagination into earthliness and became earthly, contrary to God's purpose, God's purpose nevertheless had to endure. For here God set God's purpose in Adam's child and directed God's imagination into the corrupted image. God impregnated it with God's divine power and being, and turned around the soul's will out of earthliness into God. Thus Mary became pregnant with such a child as Adam should have become pregnant with. Adam's own capacity could not do this, but instead sank down into sleep, that is, into magic. Thus, out of Adam the woman was made. She should not have been made. Rather, Adam should have impregnated himself in the matrix of Venus and given birth magically. But since this could not be, Adam was divided, and his own will of great might was shattered and closed up in death. Because he would not set his imagination in God's Spirit, his great might had to halt in death and to allow the Spirit of God to set its imagination in the might, and do with him what it wished.

Out of that same death, God's Spirit awakened life to him and became the Spirit of that same life, so that the image and likeness of God could yet be born and endure.[15] For this image stood in the virginal mirror in the wisdom of God, before the time of the world and from eternity. And the image stood in two forms, that is, in accordance with the first principle of the Father in the fire and in the second principle of the Son in the light. And yet it was revealed only in the light and in the fire as if in a magic, that is, in a possibility. Just as the starry heaven, in accordance with its capacity, models a figure to a person in one's mind in sleep, so also the image appeared in the center of the nature of fire, altogether invisibly. But in the wisdom in the mirror of the Godhead it appeared as an image, like a shadow, but without material being; yet it was in the essence of the Spirit. The Spirit, when it saw itself in the mirror of wisdom, recognized and saw this image and at once set its will into it in order to bring it into being, so that God might have an image or likeness in being, and so that God might no longer need to gaze upon God's self in a mirror but rather perceive God's self in being. And therefore when the first image imagined itself into harsh might and thereupon became earthly and dead, God's Spirit directed its will and life into death. God's Spirit took once more the first life out of death and into itself, so that the first life might endure in full obedience before God, so that God alone might be the willing and the doing.

The True Virginal Image

Thus we are to know that God entered into the half-dead image—understand this, into Mary—and into the same virginal form that lay closed up in death, in which Adam should have become pregnant and given birth to an image of himself in virginal chastity. In this closed up and half-dead virginal matrix, God's word or heart, that is, the center of the Holy Trinity, became a human image without harm to his being. And while the first living virginal matrix in Adam did not wish to be obedient to God, now it became obedient to God when it was awakened again from death, and submitted itself entirely, humbly, and willingly into God's will. Thus once again the true virginal image was now portrayed in obedience to God. For the first will had to remain in death. It had imagined contrary to God's will. And a pure obedient will was awakened, which remained in heavenly gentleness and being. It no longer allowed the image in the fire, in the Father's part, to swell up in it; rather, it remained in one quality, when the Godhead directs its life in only one quality, that is, in the light, in the Holy Spirit, and yet holds sovereignty over all three principles.[16]

And thus we are to understand concerning the incarnation of Christ. When God's Spirit reawakened in Mary the virginal life, which lay closed up in death and fierceness in the earthly essence, then this life henceforth turned itself only into one will, that is, into God's love, and submitted itself to the Spirit of God. Thus this same life became pregnant with a true virginal image. This should have been so with Adam but did not happen, for one imagination received the other. God's imagination received the imagination in death and brought it again to life, and the same life imagined once again into God and became pregnant with God, and out of the Godhead and humanity there came one person. The Godhead adhered to the heavenly being that from eternity had always been with realm, power, and glory, that is, the realm of paradise, and the angelic world, that is, the spirit and the seventh form in the center of nature.[17] And the humanity adhered to the realm of this world. But since the will of humanity submitted itself into the Godhead, this virginal image in Christ Jesus became only a guest in this world, and his Godhead was a lord over this world. For thus it should also have been in Adam, so that the lesser and powerless would have been subject to the greater and omnipotent. But Adam's will went into what was less and powerless. Therefore he became completely powerless and fell down into sleep and reverted to the creator. But with Christ this image endured in the divine being, and the earthly quality remained in the office and manner of a servant. This earthly quality was now no longer a sovereign, as it had been over Adam and Mary his mother before the high blessing and revelation of the Godhead, but a servant. For this image was now in God's Spirit and might, a sovereign over the third principle of this world.

Not a Magical Birth

Now reason says, "What happened then in this incarnation? Was the life stirred immediately at the point of conception, beyond the natural course, so that the part from Mary, that is, the woman's seed, immediately came alive?" No, for it was an essential seed and was stirred in its true natural time, with soul and spirit, like all Adam's children. But the part of the Godhead, encircled with divine being and wisdom, lived from eternity to eternity. Nothing went toward or away from the Godhead. What it was, it remained, and what it was not, it became. It gave itself with heavenly divine being into the essence and being of Mary, and Mary's essence and God's essence became one person. But Mary's essence was mortal, and God's essence was immortal. Therefore Mary's essence had to die on the cross and pass through death into life. God's essence helped this; otherwise it would not have been possible. Thus God's essence helped us and still helps us evermore through Christ's death into God's essence and life.

Thus we understand Christ's incarnation naturally, as all human children. For the heavenly, divine being has given itself with its life into the earthly, half-dead being. The sovereign yielded himself to the servant, so that the servant might become alive. He has become a complete human being in nine months, and at the same time remained a true God. He was birthed in the same way and manner of all Adam's children in this world, through the same process as all people. And thus it was, not that he needed to, for he could have been birthed magically, but he would and should heal our impure, bestial birth and entrance into this life. He was to enter into this world through our entrance and lead us out of the earthly quality.

For if he had been birthed magically in a divine way, he would not have been in this world naturally. For the heavenly being would have had to swallow up the earthly quality. Thus, if he had not been like us, how would he have wished to suffer death and enter into death and shatter it? But it is not so. He is truly the seed of the woman, and entered in this world by the natural way, like all people, but he went out through death by the divine way, in the divine power and being. It is his divine, living being that endured in death, that shattered and made a mockery of death, and that led the wounded, half-dead humanity through death into eternal life. For the earthly part that he received from his mother Mary into himself, that is, into the divine being, died to the earthly nature on the cross. Thus the soul was in God's being, and like a victorious prince led the devil into his hell, that is, into God's wrath, and extinguished it with God's love and gentleness, with the divine love-being. For the love-fire came into the wrath's fire and drowned the wrath in which the devil wished to be God. Thus the devil was taken captive by the darkness and lost his dominion. For here the sting and the sword of the cherub, of the angel of death, was shattered. And this was the reason why God became human, so that God might lead us out of death and into eternal life, and extinguish with God's love the wrath that burned within us.

Christ's Immortal Blood

For you are to understand us properly with regard to how God's wrath was extinguished. It was not with the mortal blood of Christ that he shed, concerning which the Jews mocked him. Rather, it was with the blood of the eternal life, from God's being, which was immortal and had the fountain of the water of eternal life. This was shed on the cross along with the external blood. And when the external blood fell into death, the heavenly fell with this, but it was immortal.

Thus the earth received Christ's blood. For this reason it trembled and quaked. For the fierceness of God was now overcome in the earth. And now the living blood came in it that had come from heaven, from God's being. This blood opened the graves of the saints and opened death. It made a path through death so that death was made a display of. For when Christ's body rose from death, he made a display of death in his body, for its power was shattered.

CHAPTER 11

The Most Loving Gate: Christ's Incarnation Brings Life

All of us poor children of Eve died in Adam. And even if we were alive, we lived only for this world. Death waited for us and consumed one after another. There would have been no help for us, if God had not birthed us again from God's being. We would not have come again in the body in eternity, and our soul would have remained eternally in God's wrathful quality with all of the demons. But the incarnation of Jesus Christ became a powerful being for us, because for our sakes God became human so that God could bring our humanity once more out of death and into God's self, and redeem our souls from the fire of the wrath of God. For the soul is in itself a fire-quality and contains within itself the first principle, the dry harshness, which operates in itself only as fire. So if the gentleness and love of God is withdrawn from this birth of the soul, or if it is infected with a quite harsh material, then it remains a quality in the darkness, a completely harsh roughness that devours itself and yet always gives birth to a hunger in the will. For a thing that has neither beginning nor ground also has no end. Rather it is itself its own ground; it gives birth to itself.

The Origin of the Soul

And yet we do not want to say that the soul has no beginning. It has a beginning, but only according to its creatureliness, not according to its essence. Its essence is from eternity, for the divine creative command has grasped the soul in the center of the eternal nature, and brought it into a substantial being, with the complete cross with the character of the Holy Trinity,[18] that is, as a likeness of the threefold Spirit of the Godhead, in which God dwells, whether it happens in love, or rather in light or fire. In that condition into which it imagines, it becomes pregnant, for the soul is a magic spirit, a quality within itself. The soul is the center of eternity, a fire of the Godhead in the Father, nevertheless not in the freedom of the Father, but rather in the eternal nature. The soul is not prior to the being but rather in the being. But God's freedom is outside of being, yet dwells in being. For in being, God is revealed. There would be no God without being, rather an eternal silence without quality. But in the quality, the fire is born, and out of the fire, the light is born, so that the two beings separate from each other, and bring forth two kinds of qualities, namely a fierce, hungry, thirsty quality in the fire, and a gentle, lovely, giving quality in the light. For the light gives, and the fire takes. The light gives gentleness, and from gentleness comes being, which is the food of the fire. Otherwise the light would be a dark hunger in itself, just as a spirit is if it does not have the being of light, like a languishing poison. But if a spirit receives the being of gentleness, the spirit draws being into itself and dwells therein, and needs the gentleness for food and for a body, because it infects itself with the gentleness and impregnates itself, for its being is its fulfillment, so that the hunger is quieted.

Therefore we should consider the human soul. It was taken from the center of nature, not from the mirror of the eternal, that is, from the source of this world. Rather it was taken from the eternal essence of the Spirit of God, from the first principle, from the Father's characteristic according to the nature. It is not from the being or from something, rather the Spirit of the Godhead blew life into the first human, that is, the image in Adam, one in itself, from all three principles. The Spirit of the Godhead blew the center of nature, namely the fire-quality, into the first human for life. And the Spirit of the Godhead also blew the gentleness of love from the being of the Godhead, namely the second principle with divine, heavenly being, as well as the spirit of this world, that is, the mirror and image of the wisdom of God with the miracles.

The Devil's Infection

But now the spirit of this world is corrupted with the kindling and poison of the devil, which he has thrown into the world. For the devil dwells in this world and constantly infects the outer nature and characteristic, although only in fierceness, namely dry desiring, is he mighty. However, he sets his imagination with his false transforming substance also in love, and poisons the best jewel of the soul. The devil infected Adam's soul with the devil's imagination, with his evil spirit of hunger, so that Adam's soul lusted for earthly quality, from which pleasure Adam's soul became pregnant with the earthly quality, so that the outer realm was introduced into the inner, by which the light was extinguished in the fire of the first principle. Adam's divine being, which was supposed to live eternally, was enclosed in earthly death.

God's Movement

Therefore there was no more help either for this image or for the soul, unless the Godhead would move itself according to the second principle, that is, according to the light of the eternal life in the Godhead, and would again enkindle with the radiance of love the being that had been enclosed in death. This occurred in the incarnation of Christ. This is the greatest miracle that God ever worked, that God moved God's self with the center of the Holy Trinity in the woman's seed. For God did not want to reveal God's heart in fire, that is, in the man's transforming substance, but rather in the Spirit's, namely in Venus, in the love of life, so that the fire in the man's transforming substance might be seized by the gentleness and love of God. For eternal life had to sprout again from enclosed death. Thus the root of Jesse and the true rod of Aaron sprouted and bore lovely fruits. For in Adam, paradise was closed in death when he became earthly, but in Christ paradise sprouted again out of death.

The Work and Character of Christ

From Adam we have all inherited death; from Christ we inherit eternal life. Christ is the virginal image to which Adam should have given birth from himself, with both transforming substances. But because he was not able to do this, he was divided, and had to give birth through two bodies, until Shiloh came,[19] that is, the son of the virgin, who was born of both God and a human. He is the one who breaks through, of whom the prophets spoke, who shot up as a branch.[20] He sprouted as a laurel tree in God's being. He shattered death by his entering into the human, half-dead essence. He sprouted

at the same time in the human and also in the divine essence. He
brought to us in our humanity the virginal chastity of the wisdom
of God. He encompassed our soul essence with heavenly being. He
became the hero in the combat, because the two realms lay in conflict with each other, namely between God's wrath and love. He gave
himself willingly to the wrath and thereby extinguished it with his
love. He came from God into the world, and took our soul into
himself, so that he could lead us out of the earthliness of this world
again into God in himself. He gave birth to us anew, so that we
could again be capable of living in God. From his will he gave birth
to us, so that we could put our will into him, and so he led us in
himself back to the Father into our first fatherland again, that is,
into paradise, from which Adam departed. He has become the
source of our spring, his water wells up within us. He is our spring,
and we are his drops within him. He has become the fullness of our
being, so that in him we may live in God. For God became human.
God has led God's unfathomable and immeasurable being into humanity. God has revealed God's being, which fills heaven, in humanity. Therefore the being of the human being and the being of God
have become one being, a fullness of God. Our being is God's movement in God's heaven, and we are God's children, God's miracle,
God's movement in God's unfathomable body.[21] God is Father, and
we are God's children in God. We dwell in God, and God in us. We
are God's instrument, with which God seeks and makes what God
wants. God is the fire and the light with all being. God is hidden,
and the work reveals God.

Fire and Light

Therefore we acknowledge that God is a Spirit, and God's eternal
will is magical, that is, desiring. God always creates being out of
nothing, and does so in two qualities, namely according to the fire
and the light. From the fire comes fierceness, rising, pride, which
does not want to accommodate to the light. Rather it is a fierce, seri-

ous will, according to which God is not called God but rather is called a fierce, consuming fire. This fire is not revealed in the pure Godhead. For the light has swallowed the fire and gives to the fire the light's love, its being, its water. In God's being, therefore, only love, joy, and bliss are recognized, and not fire. Rather, the fire is only a cause of the desiring will and of love, as well as of the light and of the majesty. Otherwise there would be no being, as was explained at length in the preceding writings.

The New Birth

And so we know wherein our new birth is located,[22] namely only in the imagination, so that with our wills we may enter into God's will, and completely accommodate ourselves and give ourselves over to God, which is called faith. For the word "faith" is not historical; rather it is a taking from God's being, eating from God's being, introducing God's being with one's imagination into God's soul-fire, and quieting its hunger therewith, and therefore putting on God's being, not as a garment, but rather as a body of the soul. The soul must have God's being in its fire; it must eat God's bread, if it wants to be a child.

Thus the soul is born anew in God's Spirit and being, which has transplanted the soul from the field of fierceness and wrath into the field of the love, gentleness, and humility of God. The soul blooms with a new flower, which grows up in God's love, namely in God's field. This same flower is the genuine, true image of the Godhead, which God desired when God created Adam in God's likeness, which image God has now given rebirth for us in Jesus Christ, the Son of God and of humanity. For Jesus's rebirth from God and our being is our rebirth. Christ's power, life, and spirit are all ours, and we need do nothing more than merely enter with the spirit of our will through Christ into God's being. Thus our will is born anew in God's will and receives divine power and being: not foreign power and being, rather our first power and being, with which we entered into death in Adam. The firstborn from the dead, namely Jesus

Christ, awakens this power and being to us once more. Christ is God, but is born from us, so that Christ may make us alive from the dead, not from a foreign life that we have not had here in this world. Rather this is from our own life, for God's purpose must stand: the beautiful flower and image should grow out of the corrupted field, and not that alone, but also from the pure field.

From the virgin we should be born again, and not from the man of wrath, from the transforming substance of the fire, but rather from the virgin of love and of the infused substance of light. We clothe ourselves in the virgin of Christ with our surrender. Herewith we become the virgin of modesty, chastity, and purity in the Holy Threeness in the angelic world, a mirror of the Holy Trinity in which God contemplates God's self. God has taken this virgin as a spouse. God is our husband, to whom we are married, entrusted, and embodied in Christ.[23] We are now Mary in the covenant of grace, from which God and the human are born. Mary was the first in the high blessing, for in her was the goal toward which the covenant pointed. She was known in God in the precious name of Jesus, before the foundation of the world was laid, not that she brought life out of death, rather than in her God wanted to bring life out of death. Therefore she was highly blessed, and the pure virginal chastity was put on her. And from this same virginity, from which Christ was born, we must all be born, and follow the Lamb of God, otherwise we shall not see God. For Christ says, "You must be born anew, if you want to see the realm of God, you must be born anew from water and from the Holy Spirit." The water is the virginity, for the virgin directs the transforming agent of the light and of the water, namely love and gentleness. And the Spirit, from which we should be born, is the one that gave itself over into the seed of the woman in the movement of the Godhead. This Spirit shattered death; it gave birth to a flower flaming with light, because it is the Spirit and life of the flower, not according to the fire-quality of the fierceness, but according to the quality of the light in gentleness and humility.

5

SIX MYSTICAL POINTS

A S AN AUTHOR whose works number thousands of pages, Jakob Boehme can hardly be called a man of few words. Yet at times his expression can be quite succinct. His *Six Mystical Points*, dating from 1620, is included here as an example of his terse, laconic style. The essay is placed last in this volume in the hope that the reader, after grasping the ideas presented in the foregoing chapters, will be ready to meet Boehme in his aphoristic mode.

Six Mystical Points is distinctive for its emphasis on magic. Through the lens of magic, Boehme considers some of his recurrent themes, particularly the role of desire and will in determining the shape of substance or being. Magic is concerned with transformation. Boehme describes magic as a will, the orientation that enables transformation to occur. Human life, he says, is a hinge or a pivot between light and darkness. By the direction of its desire or will, it orients its axis toward heaven or hell—unless it gives itself to neither the light-world nor the dark-world. If it yields itself "into a nothing," then it cannot burn in the fire of any particular quality. It returns to the primordial, undifferentiated unity of God's being.

Magic in itself has no distinct substance. It cannot even be said to fully exist of itself. Because it is only a will, magic is not so much substance or product as it is process. It manifests itself in the being or substance of whether it is the mother or matrix. Boehme describes magic as unknown because it stands outside of nature and creation.

Like Sophia, magic is without content, a pure mirror of desire. Unlike Sophia, magic can be used for good or for ill (in which case it becomes necromancy). Just as elements can exert an attraction to one another in alchemy, magic is desire. Thus it is the source of imagination, which directs the will into substance or being. Magic operates in all three worlds, and so enables transformation from the dark, wrathful world to the world of light and love.

Boehme explores the relationship of magic to mystery. Mystery is the magic will that can be shaped into being. A competent magician must be able to perceive the Great Mystery—the hiddenness of God—reflected in the pure mirror of Sophia. Otherwise the magician's efforts can go awry.

Boehme calls magic the "best theology" because it is the ground of true faith, just as the new birth is the foundation of genuine Christianity. Hence Six Mystical Points offers another angle of reflection on Boehme's besetting concerns. In this brief essay, alchemy meets Christian theology in a manner that is characteristic of the shoemaker and prophet of Görlitz.

PREFACE

There is no precious knowledge unless the soul once has triumphed over the attack and struck down the devil, so that it receives the garland of the knight, which the most gracious virgin of chastity sets on the soul as a sign of triumph, that the soul has triumphed in its precious knight Christ. Then arises the knowledge of wonders, but with no perfection.

THE FIRST POINT
The Blood and Water of the Soul.

Everything that is has substance and is tangible in this world. The soul is not a substance or being in this world, likewise its blood and water is not a substance or being in this world.

The Soul Is a Fire

The soul with its blood and water is indeed in the outer blood and water, but its substance is magical. For the soul is also a magical fire, and its image or form is born in the light out of the magical fire.[1] It is however a genuine image in flesh and blood, but in its primordial condition.

Just as God's wisdom has being, and yet it—wisdom—is no being, so also the soul with its image has being, and yet it—the soul—is only a magical fire. But its nourishment is from its being.

Fire and Light in Blood

Just as a fire must have being if it is to burn, so likewise the magical fire of the soul has flesh, blood, and water. For there would be no blood if the transforming substance of fire and light were not in water. The transforming substance is the essence or life of wisdom. It has in it all the forms of nature and is the other magical fire.[2]

For this transforming substance gives all colors, and out of its form goes forth the divine power, in the gentle being of the light. Understand this as in accordance with the characteristic of the light. And in accordance with the characteristic of the fire, the transforming substance is a harshness of transformation. It can lead all things to its highest level, although it is not a living spirit but rather the highest essence.

Thus also the transforming substance is such an essence in water, and introduces the characteristic of fire and of light into it, with all the powers of nature. For thus it transforms the water into blood. And it does so in the external and internal water, that is, in the external and internal blood.

The inner blood of the divine being is also magical. For magic makes it into substance. It is spiritual blood, which external being cannot move except only by imagination. The internal imagination leads the external will into the internal blood. The blood and flesh of the divine being is corrupted by this, and the noble image of the likeness of God is obscured.

The soul's flesh and blood is in the highest mystery, for they are divine being. And when the external flesh and blood die, they revert into the external mystery, and the external mystery reverts to the internal.

And every magical fire has its radiance and darkness in itself. For the sake of this, a final day of separation is appointed, when everything must pass through a fire and be tested as to what is capable [of withstanding the fire] or not. Then everything goes into its own magic and afterward is as it always was from eternity.[3]

THE SECOND POINT

The Election of Grace. Good and Evil.

From the Oneness of God to the Threeness of the Worlds

From eternity God is everything alone. God's being divides itself among three eternal distinctions. One is the fire-world, the second the dark-world, and the third is the light-world.[4] And yet it is only one being: each world is in another but none is the other.

The three distinctions are equally eternal and limitless, and bound neither in time nor place. Each distinction encloses itself as a being. And each is also its quality, in accordance with its characteristic. And in its quality is also its desire, that is, the center of nature.

And the desire is its making, for desire makes being where none is, and does so in the essence of desire, according to the characteristic of desire. And all together is only one magic, or a hunger for being.

Each form makes being in its desire, and each form leads itself out of the mirror of the form's radiance and has its seeing in its own mirror. Its seeing is a darkness for another mirror, its form is hidden to another eye, but in feeling there is a distinction.

For each form takes its feeling from the original condition of the first three forms in nature, that is, from dry, bitter, and anguish. And yet in these three there is no pain in itself, but the fire makes pain in them, and light transforms it into gentleness again.

Desire Is the Pivot between Light and Darkness

The true life stands in the fire. There is the pivot of light and darkness. The pivot is desire: with whatever it fills itself, its desire is of that fire, and its light shines out of that fire. That light is the form or seeing of that life, and the being that is led into the desire is the fire's wood. From this the fire burns, be it dry or gentle,[5] and that is also its realm of heaven or of hell.

Human life is the pivot between light and darkness. To whichever one it adapts itself, in that it burns. If it gives itself into the desire of essence, it burns in anguish, in the fire of darkness.

But if it gives itself into a nothing, then it is desireless, and reverts to the fire of light. Then it cannot burn in any quality, for it leads into its fire no being from which a fire can burn. So since there is no torment in it, the life cannot catch any torment, for there is none in it. It has reverted to the first magic, which is God in God's Threeness.

All Three Worlds in Life

When the life is born, it has all the three worlds in it. To whichever world that life adapts itself, by that it is retained, and in that fire it is enkindled.

For when the life enkindles itself, it is drawn by all the three worlds. And they are in motion in the essence, as in the first enkindled fire. Whichever essence the life invites and receives into its desire burns in that fire.

If the first essence in which the life enkindles itself is good, then the fire is also lovely and good. But if it is evil and dark, out of a fierce characteristic, then the fire is also a fierce fire, and the essence has a desire in accordance with the characteristic of the fire.

For each imagination desires only being like itself, in which it originated.

Human life in this time is like a wheel, where what is at the bottom is soon at the top. It enkindles itself in all being and soils itself with all being. But its bath is the motion of the heart of God, a water of gentleness. From this bath it can introduce being into its fire-life. The election of God does not consist in the first essence.

For the first essence is only the mystery for life. The first life with the enkindling properly belongs to its mystery, out of which it went forth. It may be a totally fierce essence, or a mixed essence, or an essence of light in accordance with the world of light.

The light of a life burns from the characteristic out of which the life first originates. This life has no election, and no judgment passes over it, for it stands in its own primordial condition and directs its judgment within. It separates itself from every other quality, for it burns only in its own quality, in its own magical fire.

Choosing Light or Darkness

Election concerns that which is invited: does it belong to the light or to the darkness? A life's will is in accordance with the life's characteristic. And the life is recognized as to whether it is of the fierce essence or of the love essence. As long as the life burns in one fire, the other leaves it alone. And the election of that fire in which it burns determines that life. For the fire wishes to have that life: it is of its characteristic.

But if that fire's will swings into another fire and enkindles itself in it,[6] then it may enkindle the whole life with that fire, if it remains in that fire.

Then the life is newly born, either to the dark-world or to the light-world, in whichever one the will has enkindled itself. Thereupon comes another election. And that is the reason why God allows people to be taught, and likewise the devil allows it. Each one wishes the life's will to swing into one's fire and to enkindle itself. And then one mystery takes hold of the other.

THE THIRD POINT
Sin. What Is a Sin, and How Is It a Sin?

Enmity Comes from Opposing Wills

A thing that is one has neither commandment nor law. But if it mixes with another thing, then there are two beings in one, and there are also two wills, one opposed to the other. There enmity arises.

Good Dies to Evil

Thus we are to regard enmity against God. God is unified and good, without any quality. Although all quality is in God, it is, however, not revealed. For the good has swallowed up the evil or opposition into itself, and holds it in constraint in the good, as imprisoned, since the evil must be a cause of life and of light, but not revealed. Instead, the good dies to the evil, so that it may dwell in the evil, without quality or perceptivity in itself.[7]

Love and enmity are only one thing; but each dwells in itself. That makes two things. Death is the boundary of separation between them, yet there is no death, except that the good dies to the evil, as the light is dead to the quality of fire and no longer feels the fire.

So now we must investigate sin in human life. For life is unified and good. But if there is another quality than good in it, then life is an enmity against God, for God dwells in the highest human life.

The Origin of Distinct Qualities

Now nothing unfathomable can dwell in something that is fathomable. For as soon as the true life awakens quality in itself, then it is not the same as the unfathomable, in which there is no quality. Thus one soon separates itself from the other.

For the good or the light is as a nothing. But if something comes into it, then this something is another thing than the nothing. For the something dwells in itself in quality. For where there is something, there must be a quality that makes and maintains the something.

Unity and Multiplicity

Thus we are to regard love and enmity. Love has but one quality and will. It desires only what is like it, and not what is manifold. For the good is only one, but quality is manifold, and the human will that desires multiplicity leads into itself, into the One,[8] the quality of multiplicity.

For the something is dark, and obscures the life's light. And the One is light, for it loves itself and has no desire for plurality.

The life's will must therefore be directed into the One,[9] and so it remains in one quality. But if it imagines another quality, it impregnates itself with the thing for which it longs.

And if this thing be without an eternal ground, in a fragile root, then it seeks a root for its preservation, so that it may continue. For every life stands in magical fire, and so every fire must have being in which it burns.

Now this same thing must make for itself being, in accordance with its desire, so that its fire has something to consume. No fire-quality can endure in the free fire, for it does not attain it, because it is only its own fire.[10]

Union with God's Will Is to Burn with God's Fire

All that is to endure in God must be free from its own will. It must not have its own fire burning in itself; rather, God's fire must be its fire. Its will must be unified in God, so that God and the human will and spirit are one.

For what is one is not at enmity with itself, for it has only one will. Wherever it goes or whatever it does, it is one with that will.

A will has only one imagination, so the imagination makes or desires only what resembles it. We are to understand similarly regarding the contrary will.

The Purpose of Law: To Return to God

God dwells in all things, and nothing understands God unless it is one with God. But if it departs from the One, it departs from God into itself, and is something other than God that separates itself. And here it is that law originates, so that it should depart again out of itself into the One. Otherwise it should be separated from the One.

Sin: To Burn in One's Own Fire

And thus it is knowable, what sin is, or how it is sin. Namely when the human will separates itself from God into a self and awakens its own self, and burns in its own quality. Then its own fire is not fit for the divine fire.

For all into which the will enters, and wishes to have as its own, is a foreign thing in the unified will of God. For all is God's, and nothing belongs to a person's own will. But if the will is in God, then everything also belongs to it.

Sin: Desire, Possessiveness, Arrogance

Thus we recognize that desire is sin. For it lusts out of one into many and leads many into one. It wishes to possess, and yet should be will-less. With the desire, being is sought, and in being the desire enkindles the fire.

Now each fire burns from the characteristic of its own being. Now separation and enmity are born. For Christ says, "Whoever is not with me is opposed to me, and whoever does not gather with me scatters" (Luke 11:23). For that person gathers outside of Christ, and what is not in Christ is outside of God.

We see, then, that greed is sin, for it is a desire outside of God. And we also see that arrogance is sin, for it wishes to be a separate self and separates itself from God, that is, from the One.

For whatever wishes to be in God must live in God, in God's will. So since we are only one in God, in many members, it is indeed in opposition to God when one member withdraws itself from the other, and makes a lord of itself, as arrogance does. Arrogance wishes to be lord, and God alone is Lord. Now there are two lords, and each separates from the other.

Therefore everything that desire possesses for itself is sin and contrary will, whether it be food or drink. If the will imagines it, then the will fills itself with it and enkindles a fire with it. Then a second fire burns in the first, and is contrary will and an error.

The Return: A New Will

Therefore out of the contrary will a new will must grow, which yields itself up again into the unified union, and the contrary will must be shattered and killed.

And here we are to ponder the word of God that became human. If one sets one's desire in this, one departs from the quality, out of one's own fire, and is newly born in the word. Thus the will that has departed dwells in God, and the first will dwells in desire, in earthli-ness, and in multiplicity.

Accordingly the multiplicity with the body must shatter and die to the will that has departed, and the will that has departed will be recog-nized as a new birth. For it takes all again into itself in the One, but not with its own desire, but rather with its own love that is unified with God, so that God may be all in all. Thus God's will may be the will of all things. For in God there is a single unified will.

So we find that evil must serve the good with respect to life, if only the will again departs out of the evil, out of itself, into the good. For the fierceness must be life's fire.[11]

But the life's will must be directed into conflict against itself, for it must flee from fierceness and not want it. It must not want desire, yet desire wants life's fire and must have it. Therefore it is com-manded to be newly born in the will.

Each will-spirit that remains in the desire of its life's fire, or en-ters into it and possesses the earthly, is separated from God as long as it possesses what is foreign.

Thus one recognizes how superfluity of food and drink effects sin. For the pure will that departs from life's fire is drowned in desire and imprisoned,[12] so that it becomes too powerless in conflict. For the quality of the fire (or of desire) holds it captive and fills it with rage, so that this will imagines desire.[13]

The will in this desire for food and drink is earthly and sepa-rated from God. But the will that escapes from the earthly fire burns in the inward fire and is divine.

This will that flees from the earthly desire does not originate from the earthly fire. No! It is the fire-will of the soul, which is cap-tured and covered by the earthly desire. It does not wish to remain in the earthly desire. Rather it wishes to enter into its One, into God, out of which it arose in the beginning.

But if it is held a prisoner in the earthly desire, then it is closed up in death and suffers torment. Thus are we to understand sin.

THE FOURTH POINT
How Christ Will Deliver
Up the Realm to His Father.

Creation: *From Fierceness to Love, Father and Son*

At the creation of the world and of all being, the Father set himself in motion in accordance with his characteristic, that is, by the center of nature, by the dark- and fire-world. This world continued in motion and dominion until the Father moved himself in accordance with his heart,[14] and God became human. Then the love of the light overcame the Father's fierce characteristic, and the Father ruled in the Son with love.

Then the Son had dominion in those that adhered to God, and the Holy Spirit drew people in the light of love,[15] through the Son, to God the Father.

The End: *The Role of the Holy Spirit*

But in the end the Holy Spirit moves in the Father's and also in the Son's characteristic, and both characteristics become active at once. And the Spirit of the Father reveals itself in fire and light, also in the fierceness of the dark-world. Then the dominion reverts to the Father. For the Holy Spirit must rule eternally, and be an eternal revealer in the light-world and also in the dark-world.

For the two worlds will stand still, and the Holy Spirit, who proceeds from the Father and Son, rules eternally in the two worlds, in accordance with each world's quality and characteristic.

The Holy Spirit alone will be the revealer of the wonders. Thus to the Father is the eternal dominion,[16] in which he rules with the Spirit.

THE FIFTH POINT

Magic. What Magic Is.
What the Magical Ground Is.

Magic and Desire

Magic is the mother of eternity, of the Being of All Beings; for it creates itself, and is understood within the context of desire.[17]

Magic in itself is nothing other than a will, and this will is the Great Mystery of all miracles and secrecy, but it leads itself by means of the imagination of the desirous hunger into being.

Magic is the primordial state of nature. Its desire makes an imagination. The imagination is only the will of desire. But desire makes in the will such a being as the will in itself is.[18]

True magic is not a being but the desiring spirit of being. Magic is an insubstantial matrix, but it reveals itself in being.[19]

Magic is spirit, and being is its body, and yet the two are only one, just as body and soul are only one person.

Magic is the greatest secrecy, for it is above nature. It makes nature in accordance with the form of its will. It is the mystery of the Three-ness. Understand this as will in the desire toward the heart of God.[20]

Magic is the forming in the divine wisdom, in which the eternal miracle of the Threeness desires to reveal itself along with nature. Magic is thus the desire that leads itself into the dark nature into fire, and through the fire, through death or fierceness, into the light toward majesty.

Magic is not majesty but rather the desire in the majesty. Magic is the desire of the divine power—not the power itself but rather the hunger or desire in the strength. It is not God's omnipotence but the director in God's power and might. The heart of God is the strength, and the Holy Spirit is the revelation of the strength.[21]

Magic is however the desire in the power and also in the direct-ing spirit; for magic has in it the creative command. What the will-spirit reveals in magic is that which magic leads into a being through the dryness, which is the creative command—all in accordance with the model of the will. As the will models in wisdom, so does the desiring magic take it in. For it has in its characteristic imagination as a delight.[22]

Imagination is gentle and soft, and it resembles water. But desire is rough and dry, as a hunger. It makes what is soft hard, and it can be found in all things, for it is the greatest being in Godhead. It leads the abyss into the foundation and the nothing into something.[23]

Magic and Understanding

In magic lie all forms of the Being of All Beings. Magic is a mother in all three worlds and makes each thing in accordance with the model of the thing's will. Magic is not the understanding, but it is a maker in accordance with the understanding and lets itself be used for good or evil.

All that the will models in knowledge—the will of understanding also enters therein—magic makes this into a being. Magic serves those who love God in God's being, for magic makes divine being in the understanding, and magic takes this out of the imagination, that is, from the gentleness of the light.

It is magic that makes divine flesh. And the understanding comes from wisdom, for understanding is a recognizer of colors, power, and virtues.[24] The understanding leads the right, true spirit with a bridle, for the spirit is soaring, and the understanding is its fire.

The spirit is not a withdrawing thing such that it deviates from the understanding; it is rather the will of the understanding. But the senses in the understanding are flying out and deviating.

For the senses are the flash out of the fire-spirit, and in the light they direct the flames of majesty into themselves, and in the darkness they direct the flash of terror, that is, a fierce flash of the fire.

The senses are such a subtle spirit, that they all give themselves into all being, and load in themselves in all being. But understanding tests everything in its fire; it rejects the evil, and keeps the good, and then magic, the mother of the good, takes the good and brings it into one being.[25]

Magic is the mother from which nature originates, and understanding is the mother originating from nature: magic leads in a fierce fire, and understanding leads its own mother, magic, out of the fierce fire into its own fire.

Understanding is the fire of power, and magic is that which burns, and yet is not to be understood as fire, rather as the power, or the mother, for the fire. The fire is called principle, and the magic is called desire.[26]

Through magic, everything is completed, good and evil. Magic's own working is necromancy and distributes itself in all characteristics. In the good, magic is good, and in the evil, it is evil. It serves children for the realm of God, and it serves the sorcerers for the devil's realm. For understanding can make of magic what it wants. Magic is without understanding, and yet comprehends everything. For magic is the concept of all things.

Magic and Learning; Philosophy and Theology

One cannot express magic's depths, for it is from eternity a ground and container of all things; it is a master of philosophy, and also a mother of the same.[27]

Philosophy leads magic, who is the mother of philosophy, according to philosophy's pleasure. Just as divine power, that is, the word, leads the harsh Father into gentleness,[28] so likewise philosophy leads its mother [magic] into a gentle divine quality.[29]

Magic is the book of all pupils. Everything that wants to learn must first study in magic, whether it be a high skill, or a lowly one. Also the farmer in the field must go to magic school, if he wants to cultivate his fields.[30]

Magic is the best theology: for in magic, true faith is grounded and found; and that person is a fool who reviles magic, for such a person does not know magic, and blasphemes God and himself or herself, and is more of a deceiver than an understanding theologian.[31]

Just like a person who fights in front of a mirror, and does not know what the fight is because one fights only outwardly, therefore in the same way the unrighteous theologian also views magic through the shining of a mirror, and understands nothing of its power. For magic is divine, and the unrighteous theologian is ungodly, even devilish, according to each characteristic of the principles. In sum, magic is the acting in the spirit of the will.

THE SIXTH POINT
Mystery: What Is It?

Mystery and Mirror

Mystery is nothing other than the magic will, which is still caught in desire, no matter how the will may form itself in the mirror of wisdom. And as the will forms itself in the transforming substance, so it will be grasped by magic and brought into a being.[32]

For the Great Mystery is nothing other than the hiddenness of the Godhead, with the Being of All Beings, from which goes forth one mystery after another. And each mystery is the mirror and image of the other, and is the great miracle of eternity, in which all things are enclosed, and will be seen from eternity in the mirror of wisdom. And nothing happens, unless it has been known from eternity in the mirror of wisdom.[33]

However, you must understand according to the characteristics of the mirror, according to all forms of nature, that is, according to light and darkness, according to comprehensibility and incomprehensibility, according to love and wrath, according to light and fire.[34]

Magic Is a Power for Good or Ill

In this same mystery, the magician has power to act in accordance with his or her will, and can do whatever he or she wants.

But the magician must be armed in the same being, in which he or she wants to act, or else the magician will be cast out as a foreigner and will be given over to the spirits of the same being in their force, for them to deal with according to the magician's desires. Concerning this, nothing more will be mentioned here, because of the chaos.[35]

Notes

Introduction

1. *Epistle* 12. See note 8 below for the source of Boehme's works.
2. *Aurora*, chapter 19.
3. *Clavis*, chapter 4.
4. *The Threefold Life of Humankind*, chapter 16.
5. *The Threefold Life of Humankind*, chapter 5.
6. This is an example of Boehme's use of the language of nature, in which each syllable of a word has its own meaning.
7. *The Signature of All Things*, chapter 3.
8. All our translations are from Johann Georg Gichtel's 1730 Leipzig edition of Jakob Boehme's work, *Theosophia revelata: Das ist: Alle göttliche Schriften des gottseligen und hocherleuchteten deutschen Theosophi Jacob Böhmens* (Amsterdam, 1730).
9. *The Incarnation of Jesus Christ*, part 2, chapter 7.

Chapter 1. Life Beyond the Senses

1. *The Great Mystery*, chapter 30, paragraph 42.
2. His reference to the cherub's sword is from chapter 3 of Genesis, where after expelling Adam and Eve from the Garden of Eden, God places cherubim with flaming swords to guard the way to the tree of life. These cherubim are not the harmless,

half-clothed baby angels from contemporary Christmas cards; they are fierce, terrifying creatures.

3. Here Boehme contrasts the life beyond the senses with the life that is perceived with the senses. Life perceived only through human sensing is figurative, a life experienced only in images. Such a life is inferior to the life experienced in the ground of God, where our sensing is divinely guided. When we participate in the divine essence, nothing can harm us; we are beyond images. It is through images and other sensory data that evil seeks to entice our wills. The apophatic way may seem austere, but it is safe.

4. Although we may think that we control taking possession of things, Boehme points out how easily things possess us. For Boehme, the goals of the spiritual life include freedom from servile attachment to things and freedom to be possessed by God, and awareness of God working in and through us. The soul's mind is the *Gemüth*, the rational faculty of the soul, which contrasts with human reason or intellect (*Vernunft*), which is easily misled, Boehme says, into self-deception.

5. The answer of the teacher conflates at least two parts of verses from the Gospel according to John. The first clause, "If you remain in my word," echoes John 8:31, while the second clause, "my words will remain in you," echoes John 15:8.

6. The problem is not materiality, but the danger that our desires might enslave the will. Like Paul, Boehme is an apostle of freedom. Although Boehme uses the strong word "hate," the purpose is not for self-destruction, but to direct the will toward rest, rather than the anguish of unsatisfied desires.

7. In the life beyond the physical senses, one instead experiences the spiritual senses.

8. Contrary to a worldly culture of self-indulgence, the cross is an occasion for joy. In the life beyond the senses, love transforms how one perceives.

9. A textual variant has "life" rather than "body."

10. Love's duty (*Amt*, translated here as "official charge") is to find a place of silence amid the constant images produced by human desires. When love finds such a place, it takes charge and burns with a joyous, raging fire. Like an alchemist's refining fire, love removes all self-constructed images.

11. In times of anguish, love intensifies its fire. Here Boehme uses the image of an alchemist forcing air onto a fire with bellows.

12. The metaphor of fabric may be inspired by Boehme's occupation as a linen merchant, which he had entered by this time. *Wirken* can mean "to work" or "to weave." Boehme may be playing with both meanings in discussing the exterior person and the interior life.

13. With "figure," Boehme implies that these people are involved in the appearance but not in the substance of the struggle between good and evil. Vain theological dispute is selfish, and such strife can serve destructive purposes. As Boehme has argued, life beyond the senses is a life beyond possessiveness and is peaceful and loving, not violent and dominating.

14. Boehme refers to 2 Cor. 13:13.

Chapter 2. The New Birth

1. The preface to *The New Birth* has been omitted from the body of this translation, because in the preface Boehme mostly refers to other writings of his that are not contained in this volume.

2. This is not, strictly speaking, a Calvinist understanding of a spiritual apprehension of Christ during the Lord's Supper. Neither is it exactly a Schwenkfeldian understanding of spiritual presence with no external practice of the Lord's Supper. However, Boehme was subject to accusations from his orthodox Lutheran opponents of being a Calvinist or a Schwenkfelder.

3. A textual variant adds "in Christ."

4. The phrase "If you would keep account of sin, no living person is righteous in your presence," combines allusions to Psalm 143:2

("And do not enter into judgment with your servant, for no living person is righteous in your presence") and to Psalm 130:3 ("If you, Lord, should reckon sins, Lord, who would endure?").

5. A textual variant adds "and sinful."

6. The word translated as "vanity" can also mean "futility."

7. The phrase "the light shines in the darkness, and the darkness does not grasp the light" refers to John 1:5.

8. The word *Recht*, translated as "rights," also means "autonomy." Likewise the word *Gewalt*, here rendered as "power" but often translated as "force," also has legal connotations of "authority" or "dominion." Boehme alludes to legal language of rights and autonomy in referring to the light and darkness. We may hear an echo of the Thirty Years' War, where princes of the three major religions sought to take control of more territory, limiting the rights and autonomy of the inhabitants. Boehme hoped for a solution that permitted religious tolerance rather than domination.

9. Manuscripts differ here; some have *limus* and others *limbus*. Elsewhere in his writings, Boehme uses these terms in wordplay. *Limbus* is a "border" and *limus* is "mud" or "slime." Boehme did not really know Latin, so he may have understood *limus* simply as "earth," since that is how Luther translated it in the Creation story in Genesis. *Limus* is the word used in the Latin Vulgate to describe the material (*limus terrae*) from which God created Adam. Boehme describes a sequence of materials: the body made of the mud of the earth, which was made of the dark-world and the light-world, out of which the human emerges through God's creative utterance (*Verbo Fiat*).

10. This divine breath derives from all three worlds. The first three characteristics of the breath of understanding comes from the fire-world. The breath is life-giving because its power comes from transformation.

11. The word translated here as "gentleness" can also mean "meekness" (used in the German translation of the beatitude in Matthew 5:5, "Blessed are the meek for they shall inherit the earth").

12. Some manuscripts have "mud" (*limus*) while others have "border" (*limbus*).

13. Elsewhere in this treatise *Fiat*, which here seems best rendered as "creative power," is translated as "creative command."

14. The realm of joy includes human playfulness and divine playfulness. This passage shows Boehme's own playfulness and his genius in the richness of his language, which evokes multiple meanings. He suggests that the soul can be both a musical instrument and a tool, on which or with which God works and plays. By referring to harmony, Boehme conveys a sense of inner harmony of the soul with God, a harmony of the created order and musical harmony. As in English, "play" connotes both the creation of music and the playfulness that God's Spirit enjoys in the spiritual life.

15. A textual variant for "world" is "quality."

16. The phrase translated as "digestive system" is literally "maggot sack," Boehme's derogatory expression for the digestive organs. He believed that in the primeval, angelic state, Adam and Eve did not need to digest or eliminate because their angelic, crystalline bodies absorbed paradisaical food magically.

17. A textual variant adds "with the soul within it."

18. In an internalized apocalypse—compare Revelation 4:1—the trumpet calls people to come up. Boehme calls his readers to come out of vanity, for through vanity the grim fire-world, the inner hell, was awakened.

19. A textual variant has "loathsome" for "vain."

20. A textual variant has "behind" for "under."

21. This may be an allusion to the earthquake after the death of Christ, found in Matthew 27:51.

22. After the fall into sin, the humans could no longer derive nutrition from any of the fruits of paradise, which all had magical qualities. In Genesis, God's curse means humans must toil for food. Boehme interpreted the curse differently, to show that God ended the heavenly nutritive value of the fruits.

23. Boehme's comment about pearls cast before beasts echoes Matthew 7:6.

24. A textual variant has "vain" (*Eitel*) in place of "something loathsome" (*Eckel*).

25. The crushing of the serpent's head refers to Genesis 3:15, a text that Boehme, concurring with the Christian understanding that had long preceded him, read as foreshadowing the Second Coming of Christ.

26. The word of God awakens in Mary's seed what faded from Adam. The word does not cause Jesus to have an angelic body, such as the one that Adam originally had. But it does restore the fadedness in Mary's seed, so that the humanity of Jesus is centered in love rather than wrath.

27. For the rod of Aaron, see Numbers 17:8. A textual variant adds "and the true high priest."

28. For consistency's sake, we have retained "being." Some might suggest that "substance" is a more suitable word, since it is here identified with embodiment and corporeality.

29. "Equilibrium" (*Concordantz*) is a musical term, along with "harmony." Boehme frequently uses musical terms in his description of heavenly life.

30. A textual variant adds "in this time" after the word "yet" in the first sentence.

31. A textual variant adds "corrupted."

32. A textual variant adds "which will mock the will because it has left its own house in which it was born."

33. A textual variant adds "Christ's heavenly corporeality, which fills the Father to all extents, and is near to all, and is through all."

34. "She" can refer to Sophia, the heavenly Wisdom, who will appear below. Johann Georg Gichtel, Boehme's editor, believed this to be the case, as he describes in his summary for chapter 4 in the 1685 edition. "She" could also refer to the great love or the heavenly food mentioned above.

35. A textual variant adds to the end of this sentence "therefore she is called Sophia, that is, the bride of Christ."

36. This sentence echoes Galatians 5:17.

37. A textual variant has "earthly."

38. The last word is literally "flute."

39. "The devil also knows that there is one God" may echo James 2:19: "You believe that there is one God, and you are right; the demons also believe it and tremble."

40. The source for Ishmael mocking is Genesis 21:9.

41. Genesis 22 contains the story of Abraham on Mount Moriah.

42. Boehme calls Adam the father of Ishmael. In the biblical account, it was Abraham who sired Ishmael with Hagar, but Boehme understands Ishmael allegorically as the offspring of the rebellious Adam. See chapter 2 of *True Yieldedness* later in this volume.

43. This passage echoes the language of Paul. See Galatians 3:27, Colossians 3:10, and Romans 13:14.

44. The phrase "gain a form in us" is from Galatians 4:19.

45. A textual variant has "worth" for "way."

46. A textual variant adds "and of vanity."

47. Boehme makes an unusual statement at the end of the paragraph by speaking of *bruederliche Versoehnung* (translated here as "fraternal and sororal reconciliation") in connection with absolution among the church's other sacraments of the word and the bread and cup. One might expect absolution grounded in the word and/or the minister. The description of brotherly and sisterly absolution sounds a different tone, reminiscent of Anabaptists.

48. Boehme often uses the word "testament" to refer to sacrament.

49. The phrase "biting about the husks" means "arguing about mere externals."

50. Boehme's strong imagery is drawn from the biblical prophets, who speak of faithlessness to God in terms of marital unfaithfulness. The image of the Whore of Babylon comes from the book of Revelation.

51. Here Boehme also paraphrases John 11:26 and John 7:38.

52. Here Boehme refers to John 13:35 and John 15:17.

53. Some manuscripts omit the phrase "that we learn it."

54. Boehme believes that while argumentative people are out-growths of the devil's work, they serve for good because the children of God bear fruit under tribulation.

55. Boehme here echoes Isaiah 26:16, in Luther's Bible.

56. A textual variant has "being" instead of "fragile life."

57. A textual variant has the "false shepherd's" instead of "his."

58. The German text has *luesterende*, "lusting," but the context suggests that this is a typographical error for *laesterende*, "slanderous."

Chapter 3. True Yieldedness

1. Johannes Tauler, *Die Predigten Taulers. Aus der Engelberger und der Freiburger Handschrift sowie aus Schmidts Abschriften der ehemaligen Straßburger Handschriften*, ed. Ferdinand Vetter (Berlin: Weidmann, 1910), http://mhgta.uni-trier.de/katalog suche.php?ses_id=260b5b9efdb8ba908cb3427213326c84&suc hwort=tauler&ordnung=fbsigle&gesendet=Suchen (accessed March 25, 2008).

2. The word translated here as "wise" could also mean "cunning" or "shrewd," but its use in Genesis 3:6 suggests that "wise" is the connotation here.

3. A textual variant adds "which is however only a mirror of the eternal."

4. A textual variant adds "namely in the darkness of the self, in the outward light of reason."

5. A textual variant adds "in its darkness, indeed, in its avarice."

6. A textual variant adds "as can be seen in Revelation."

7. Unlike the other subheadings, which are additions by the edi-tors of the present volume, this subheading appears in the 1730 edition of Boehme's work. The Latinate word *Processus* in the subtitle, translated here as "process," is an alchemical term.

8. A textual variant adds "which rises with reason in the light of God, from which the soul ought to eat and revive itself."

9. By "robber castle" Boehme is referring to the plundering rogue knights (*Raubritter*) who terrorized the countryside with their highway robbery, and retreated with their stolen treasure to their fortresses. This was a form of organized crime in Boehme's era.

10. The phrase "useless carving" may be an echo of the "carved idol" that is forbidden in the Ten Commandments.

11. The term "child-state" (*Kindschaft*) echoes Galatians 4:5 and Romans 8:23 and 9:4, and is often translated "adoption" in modern versions.

12. Concerning the phrase "in and for hell," the German word *ins* means both "in" and "for," but English requires two words to imply purpose and location. Again, the word translated as the devil's "mother" can also mean "matrix."

13. A textual variant reads "the devil has no more might, except in the great chaos."

14. The source of "Abba, dear Father, deliver me from evil" is Matthew 6:13.

15. A textual variant adds "although it may happen that the earthly will becomes too strong in God's fierceness through the devil's excessive rage."

16. The source of the phrase "are called according to the purpose" is Romans 8:28.

17. The phrase "Christ has given us the might to become God's children" echoes John 1:12.

18. The phrase "God will not cast out" refers to John 6:37.

19. A textual variant reads "and should be, with Christ's death, sovereign over the death of sin."

20. The passage from Galatians speaks of Abraham. As elsewhere, Boehme regards Abraham as figuratively representing Adam. See, for example, chapter 5 of *The New Birth*.

21. The phrase "Cast out the female servant's son, for he must not inherit with the free woman" refers to Genesis 21:10.

22. For more on the feminine quality of Christ, see the chapters from *The Incarnation of Jesus Christ*, included later in this volume.

23. Readers of the Bible in English are accustomed to earthly "tabernacle" or "tent," as for example in 2 Corinthians 5:1, but Boehme's Bible had "hut."

24. A textual variant reads "is a futile, worthless consolation."

25. This sentence refers to Matthew 6:22.

26. The sarcastic tone of Boehme's expression "soiled block of wood" is difficult to translate. Literally it is a soiled piece of wood, but "wooden" can mean lifeless or dumb, as in English. "Stick in the mud" may capture some but not all of this colorful phrase.

27. See Mark 4:31.

28. The phrase "until Christ takes a form" refers to Galatians 4:19.

29. Herod's infanticide can be found in Matthew 2:16.

30. The phrase "the sensual pleasure of the flesh and the arrogant life" refers to 1 John 2:16.

31. Thoughtful Christians in later periods have abandoned the practice of blaming "the Jews" for the crucifixion.

32. Note how this final sentence with its plant imagery echoes the end of the first chapter of this treatise.

Chapter 4. The Incarnation of Jesus Christ

1. For Boehme, *Menschwerdung*, translated here as "incarnation," has more layers of meaning than just taking on human flesh. For Boehme, becoming human involved a wide range of complex properties of human existence. We've retained the term "incarnation" because it was the typical German word used for the Latin *incarnatio*.

2. The word translated as "chaos" is *Turba*. The word translated as "creative command" is *Fiat*, which means literally, "Let there be." It is the expression used in the Latin Vulgate Bible in the first chapter of Genesis when God creates by divine command. Ether is the material that fills space beyond the clouds and beyond the moon's realm. It was also understood to fill the spaces between

the planets and stars, as well as between particles on earth.

3. The blessing refers to the Annunciation, when the angel Gabriel greeted Mary and revealed to her that she was to be the mother of Jesus.

4. Some manuscripts read "corrupted" rather than "hidden."

5. Some manuscripts add "that God wished to reveal again the eternal virginity."

6. The phrase "works of the law" refers to Israel's keeping the commandments of the covenant, the laws of Moses.

7. Some manuscripts add "as a lord and conqueror of the quality."

8. The phrase "water of eternal life" refers to John 4:14.

9. In the phrase "She carried the word of life in her body," the word translated as "body" can often mean "womb." The latter may be more biologically accurate, but "body" is echoed below in another context.

10. "In eternity," as opposed to time, it is not to be forgotten that in her, God became human.

11. In the Gospel according to John, Jesus is in conflict with the leaders of the Jewish community, often referred to simply as "the Jews." Tragically, the use of this term in John has been used to justify much Christian anti-Semitism.

12. By Holy Threeness (*Ternarium Sanctum*), Boehme is referring to the Christian doctrine of the Trinity, but also to his own unique teachings on the three principles or three worlds.

13. Some manuscripts add "encircled with the heavenly and chaste Virgin of Wisdom dwelling in the heavenly being."

14. Some manuscripts read "The living being came into the half-killed essence of Mary and took the half-killed essence for a body."

15. Some manuscripts add "from eternity so recognized in God's wisdom."

16. At the end of this paragraph, Boehme shifts to the present tense because he is talking about God, whose activity is ongoing.

17. Here Boehme adds a reference to one of his other writings, "as

has been recounted in full detail in the third section of our book *The Threefold Life of Humankind*."

18. Here Boehme inserted a figure of a cross rather than the written word.

19. Genesis 49:10 is the biblical source of the reference to Shiloh.

20. Here Boehme refers to Isaiah 53:2.

21. When Boehme speaks of the movement becoming God's body, it may be possible that a misspelling has occurred and Boehme actually meant God's love (*Liebe*, rather than *Leibe*).

22. A textual variant adds "because in this world we are covered with these earthly huts, and have reverted to the earthly life."

23. The word translated as "embodied" can mean also "incorporated." The phrase echoes Paul's comments that by faith we are incorporated into Christ, as, for example, in Galatians 3:26–28.

Chapter 5. Six Mystical Points

1. A textual variant adds "in the power of its own fire and light."

2. In Boehme's alchemical understanding, fire and light become fluid if suspended in water. They become blood of a spiritual or physical sort. His thought here may also be influenced by the notion in the scriptures that life is in the blood.

3. Like the alchemist's fire, this fire separates the pure from the base. It purifies and transmutes.

4. Here Boehme is not consistent with his usual language. Here the dark-world is the visible world.

5. The word translated as "dry" here can also mean "harsh."

6. A textual variant adds "that is, the turning pivot."

7. Good must die to evil so that it may live within the evil, without being corrupted in its quality by the evil.

8. A textual variant adds "in which God dwells."

9. A textual variant adds "that is, into the good."

10. It cannot withstand a quality-free fire because it has no fuel. Such a fire-quality cannot endure a quality-free fire because it is its own fire.

11. Evil serves good by having fury become fuel for the fire of life.

12. A textual variant adds "that is, in the fierceness of the wood for fire."

13. A textual variant adds "that is, the earthly."

14. A textual variant adds "and the light-world."

15. A textual variant adds "that proceeds from the Father and Son."

16. After "the Father," a textual variant adds the phrase "who is all."

17. Here it may be useful to recall that the word translated "mother" can also mean "matrix." Desire is the catalyst of transformation.

18. The will sees itself like a reflection in a mirror—recall the role of Sophia. All exists at all times in all things. The imagination therefore situates the will to perceive (or even to be, to exist) in the particular condition or characteristic that it desires—whether it be the love principle or the wrath principle.

19. Magic has no substance, but it has spirit. It manifests itself in the being or substance of that of which it is the origin or mother.

20. Magic is unknown because it stands outside of nature and creation. It is the driving orientation of creation. "Threeness" recalls the Trinity within the Godhead, the three principles (the three worlds), and the alchemical triad of mercury, sulfur, and salt.

21. There is an echo of the Threeness of God in this passage: might is reminiscent of the Father, the love in the heart of God is the Son, and the revealer is the Spirit.

22. Dryness (*Herbigkeit*) is, among other things, the tendency to contract or withdraw into itself. This quality enables beings to have separate existence, so it is essential to creation. It is a creative capacity and the means by which objects take shape. The word translated as "creative command" is the Latin term *Fiat*, the "Let there be" of creation in Genesis 1. The phrase "as the will models in wisdom" echoes the language of Proverbs 8, where wisdom is the architect for creation. See Proverbs 8:22

following, especially verse 30, which in Jakob Boehme's German Bible (Luther's translation) reads thus: "I (Wisdom) was God's delight (*Lust*) and played before God always; I played in God's orb and had my delight in humankind."

23. Desire is attraction and also contraction. It gives concrete shape to the pliant, fluid imagination.

24. Magic and understanding informed the creation of the primordial Adam, who had (in his prematerial, unearthly state) extraordinary powers of perception, as he also did in kabbalistic teaching.

25. The senses are a lightning for the fire-spirit, and bring with them the flame (i.e., light) of the majesty of God. This paragraph suggests that as such, they are subtle, and capable of entering into being and bearing being. That is to say, not only do they contribute to perceiving light along with fire, but they may themselves participate in being. The senses, and their participation in being, contrast with understanding, which is another kind of fire: one for testing. When understanding can test for good and evil and can reject evil, then understanding can grasp magic (see below) and can join it in being.

26. Understanding steers magic toward either good or evil.

27. By this reference to the academic degree, Boehme may be having fun at the expense of his more educated contemporaries.

28. A textual variant adds "or heart of God."

29. A textual variant adds "that is, understanding."

30. Boehme's reference to the farmer is most likely not literal. Such a person could be someone who understands good theology as magic, or a practitioner of white magic, or someone who has experienced the new birth.

31. The word translated here as "deceiver" was also used in Boehme's day to refer to a charlatan alchemist.

32. By "transforming substance" here, Boehme means whatever brings the will into its final form. In metallic process, the trans-

forming substance helps to process the new metal, making transformation possible.

33. The Godhead as Being of All Beings is hidden; this is the Great Mystery, giving rise to a series of mysteries that reflect one another. This mystery is beyond time (the miracle of eternity), and it encompasses all things. Although hidden, the Great Mystery is reflected into the "mirror" of Wisdom or Sophia. Through heavenly Wisdom, one may perceive reflections of the Great Mystery of the Godhead.

34. A textual variant adds "as is mentioned in other places."

35. The magician must be cautious about the realm of being in which he or she wishes to work with magic. If the magician is not well prepared ("armed") then the spirits of that realm of being will reject this person. The outcome may not be pleasant, and Boehme provides no further comment because of the commotion or uproar (*Turba*) that such a process would unleash. *Turba* can mean "a crowd of people" (or "spirits," in Boehme) and can also mean the chaos, tumult, or disturbance (like a riot) that such a crowd creates when they become unruly. *Turba* here probably refers to the disturbance created by the spirits when an incompetent magician seeks to work in a realm that the magician does not understand.

Bibliography

Primary Sources

The edition of Boehme's works used for this anthology is generally considered to be the critical edition.

Böhme, Jacob. *Sämtliche Schriften.* Edited by Will-Erich Peuckert and August Faust. 11 vols. Stuttgart: Fr. Frommanns Verlag, 1955–1961. It is a facsimile reprint of Gichtel's critical edition of 1730: *Theosophia Revelata. Das ist: Alle Göttliche Schriften des gottseligen und hocherleuchteten deutschen Theosophi Jacob Böhmens.* Edited by Johann Georg Gichtel and Johann Wilhelm Ueberfeld. Amsterdam, 1730.

Boehme's works were first fully translated into English by John Sparrow in the 1640s and 1650s. In the early 2000s, Kessinger Publishing reprinted Boehme's works, mostly by reprinting Sparrow's translations. In the case of *Von der Menschwerdung Jesu Christi*, Kessinger used John Rolleston Earle's translation from 1934. Sparrow's translations obviously are in Elizabethan English, which is less helpful for comprehending Boehme today. As of this writing, Sparrow's translation is the only translation of Boehme's complete works into English.

Boehme, Jacob. *Incarnation of Jesus Christ.* Translated by John Rolleston Earle. London: Constable, 1934.

_____. *The Way to Christ.* Translated by Peter C. Erb. New York: Paulist Press, 1978.

Secondary Literature

Brinton, Howard H. *Mystic Will: Based Upon a Study of the Philosophy of Jacob Boehme.* New York: Macmillan, 1930. Reprinted by Kessinger Publishing, 1994.

Buddecke, Werner. *Die Jakob Böhme Ausgaben. Ein beschreibendes Verzeichnis.* 2 vols. Göttingen: Häntzschel, 1937/1957.

Stoudt, John Joseph. *Sunrise to Eternity: A Study in Jacob Boehme's Life and Thought.* Philadelphia: University of Pennsylvania Press, 1957.

Versluis, Arthur, translator and editor. *The Wisdom of Jacob Böhme.* St. Paul, Minn.: New Grail, 2003.

Weeks, Andrew. *Boehme: An Intellectual Biography of the Seventeenth-Century Philosopher and Mystic.* Albany: State University of New York Press, 1991.

_____. *German Mysticism from Hildegard of Bingen to Ludwig Wittgenstein: A Literary and Intellectual History.* Albany: State University of New York Press, 1993.

Index

reason and, 102, 103, 109
reconciled to God through divine love,
  59
sin and, 63
where they dwell, 45, 46, 51, 59, 63, 69,
  102, 103, 112, 146
will and, 44, 46, 113
See also Lucifer and Adam; Satan
domination and lust for dominion, 96
drunkenness, 102–3
dying
  in Christ's death, 118–19
  See also death

earthly quality. *See* heavenly and earthly
  qualities
Eden. *See* Adam; Fall
ego. *See* arrogance; I-ness; self; vanity
elements, four (alchemical), 18, 65, 136
  origins, 67
  See also alchemy
Emmanuel
  Christ and, 86, 138
  gate of, 129
enmity, 157–58
  as coming from opposing wills, 157
Esau, 81
Eternal One, 40, 47. *See also* God
eternity, 64–66
Eve, 7, 14, 73, 132, 133
  creation of, 7, 70–72
  See also Adam; forbidden fruit
evil, 111–12
  God wills no, 116–17
  See also good and evil

fadedness of being, 73–77
faith, 93, 127–28, 149
  nature of, 77
  need for true, 122
  new birth and, 125, 126
Fall (in Eden), 7, 58–59, 129, 132–33
  sexual differentiation as consequence
    of, 31
false Babel, 103
false Christians, 87. *See also* Christians
  in name only vs. real Christians;
  mouth-Christians
false desire. *See* desire: false
false imagination, 102–3

false transforming substance, 146
false will. *See* will: false
female servant (New Testament), 80
  son of, 81, 117–19
fierceness. *See* fire; wrath
fire, 9, 10, 21
  in blood, 153–54
  burning with God's, 159
  light and, 148–49
  in the light vs. the darkness, 66 (*see also
    under* light)
  sin and burning in one's own, 159
  soul as a, 153
  transforming substance of, 71, 135, 150,
    153
  water and, 65, 69, 149
  See also love: fire of
fire-soul/outer person vs. inner person,
  78–80
flesh and blood, 36, 45, 59–60
  of Christ, 52, 62, 77, 85, 86, 138
  of soul, 153–54
  spiritual, 31, 49
  See also body; resurrection
forbidden fruit, 7, 58–59, 72–73, 96
forgiveness. *See* absolution
Franckenberg, Abraham von, 2
free will, 54. *See also* will
freedom, 21, 22
friends, 39
fruit. *See* forbidden fruit; paradise: fruit of

Garden of Eden. *See* Adam; Fall
Gelassenheit, 8, 95–96. *See also* yieldedness
gender, 15
  all of one, 49–50 (*see also* androgyny;
    male and female: union of)
gentleness, 146
giving and receiving, 93
glorification, 50
God, 7
  as androgynous, 13, 14
  becoming a child of, 115–16
  breath of, 67, 68
  heart of, 131, 134, 137, 139, 141, 156, 163
  how to hear and see, 33
  humans created in image and likeness
    of, 67–69, 115, 129–30, 140–41, 149
  living in, 160
  movement of, 147

Printed in the United States
By Bookmasters